Working Things Out

WORKING THINGS OUT

**STEVE HOLLAWAY
and BILL JUNKER**

BROADMAN PRESS
Nashville, Tennessee

Scripture quotations marked "TLB" are taken from *The Living Bible, Paraphrased* (Wheaton: Tyndale House Publishers, 1971) and are used by permission.

Scripture quotations marked "Phillips" are from *The New Testament in Modern English,* © J. B. Phillips, 1958. Used with permission of The MacMillan Company.

Scripture quotations marked "NEB" are from *The New English Bible, New Testament,* Second Edition. © The Delegates of the Oxford University Press, and the Sundics of the Cambridge University Press 1961, 1970. Reprinted by permission.

And thanks to . . .

Harry Kruener, Andrew Lester, Robert Hamill, and the late Kyle Haselden for their referred-to thoughts and for other helpful ideas not attributed to them in the text.

Library of Congress Catalog Card Number: 74-76913
Printed in the United States of America

Steve: To Wini Smith,
my teacher,

Bill: and to Patsy Junker,
my encourager,

Bill and Steve: and to Christian students
with courage enough
and love enough
to grapple with hard questions.

Contents

1 The Question Mark Inside

Steve

If you've been to college, you know the feeling.

If you're going, you'll find out what it's like.

It's the question mark inside—gnawing, growing to fill every empty spot. You're on campus, sitting alone (you seem to sit that way more often now), looking at the trees and the concrete and the people you still haven't met. The leaves are falling and the bridges are falling and you want to cross over this one place, but you are stopped dead by the voice asking, *Why am I here?*

It sounds silly if you ask it out loud. It sounds like you've been thinking too much. The shadow in the glass says, *Look, man, if you didn't think about it, we'd have some fun.* The shadow in your heart says, *Why am I here?* For a long time maybe you stare at your hands or at a wall or at a blank page. After a long time you realize that the question is important, that it is many questions. Maybe, if you're fortunate, you get down on your knees and talk to God about it. And maybe, after a long time, you find an answer for yourself and you think, *This is what college is about.*

That's what this book is about: questions and answers and college. We're trying to talk about some of the questions you have to deal with when you go through college as a Christian. We're not playing *Answer Man*. One of us is still in college, still struggling with questions and blank pages and friends. Perhaps I can talk to you like a friend, maybe like a brother. The other of us is the father of an almost-college student and has given the largest part of his professional life to publishing for and trying to figure out college students. We don't pretend to have complete answers, but we can at least point you in a Christian direction.

It's important to decide what the questions are. There's no way you're going to read this book and say, "Here are the answers to all my questions!" We don't hope for that. If you're already in college, we just hope a silent voice will say, *Yes, yes, that's how it is.* We hope you'll show a paragraph to your roommate and say, "Here, this is what we're talking about." If you're getting ready for college, we think we'll help you know what to expect, so that when a big, bad question comes knocking at your dormitory door, you'll say: "Oh, it's just you. I was expecting you." Don't shut the door in his face. He deserves an answer.

Bill

It may sound as if survival is your greatest job on campus. In truth it may be, if by "survival" you mean "emergence" as the person God intends you to be.

Many types of evangelists are abroad, hawking their wares. Many gods of the campus are being extolled and worshiped—success, coolness, intellect, power. Each of these gods has its appeal. Each would have you settle for an inferior, narrow goal for your life. But God is calling you to recognize, develop, and use all the gifts he has given you . . . for your own sake and for the good of others.

With God active in your life, calling you and helping you to be your best, you can count on surviving . . . and much more. The apostle Paul predicted the future for all those who choose to live with God on the frontier of life: "Things beyond our seeing, things beyond our hearing, things beyond our imagining, all prepared by God for those who love him" (1 Cor. 2:9, NEB).

2 How Can I Know the Will of God in College?

Steve

College is a time of making decisions about what you want and about what God wants. Even in picking freshman courses, you're making a commitment to a vocational area and a whole way of life. With every step, two roads diverge, and taking one path or another can make all the difference.

Say you've got to fulfill a science requirement as a freshman. You can take an easy geology course offered primarily for athletes, or you can take a tough biology course offered primarily for premeds. If you pick "Rocks for Jocks" instead of the bio course, your chances of entering the health profession become pretty slim. By the time you pick your major, you're really into *Crucial Decisions*. It gets pretty scary, with or without God. If you aren't seeking God's will, you've got no basis for making such a decision. If you *are* seeking his will, the decision seems even more crucial to you; and the consequences of a wrong choice seem even more tragic.

Things sometimes get to where you have to trust God. After all, God has made a lot more decisions than you have, and he made a lot of decisions about the way he made you. When I'm thinking about God's will, I sometimes think of myself as shapeless putty I can make into anything I please. I forget that I already *am* somebody. God has already made most of the decisions about what I am. He's given me all sorts of potentials and limitations, and it's up to me to find out what they are and to use the potentials and limitations for God.

I used to think that the will of God was a complex blueprint locked away in heaven, that it was the craziest blueprint imaginable, that you couldn't guess it in a million years. It had to drop out of the sky at you and catch you by surprise, or it couldn't be the real thing. This idea came from the false notion that God only worked through miracles perceived by the heart, never the mind, and that therefore whatever was reasonable was false.

"Stephen," my friends would say to me, "We could have figured out by common sense that God wants you to write; the idea must have come from your mind, so it must be selfish and wrong. Maybe he wants you to be a jungle doctor or something." I've known people who tried to determine God's will by deciding what they were *not* good at. Someone who was a terrible speaker would say, "Oh, the Lord must be going to call me to preach because everyone will see that it's the Lord speaking and not me."

All of this is reasoning from the assumption that God made us in an absurd way. It is saying that God gave us gifts we are not to use and gave us deficiencies just so we could change them. This method of vocational choice may be really a form of showing off. When a person tries to find God's will by a leap of faith into the absurd, he is sometimes merely showing off his leaping ability; and he is saying to his Christian friends, "While you have to rely on your *natural* talents, I am relying on God for *spiritual* abilities." This is plain stupid and unbiblical.

The Bible teaches that God creates us with gifts which he demands that we use. I hope you don't *really* believe that you shouldn't use your mind. You might as well cut out half your brain and live as a retarded saint. God gave you a sound mind, and if you bury it in the sand—as the servant did in Jesus' parable of the talents—he will cast you out into eternal darkness. That would be quite a leap, indeed.

12

We already know a lot about the will of God because we have his commandments. We know that God wills for us to love one another. This fact may lead some people to ask, "Why do you keep asking about God's will? You already know it." But you know, and I know, that we need something more than that; we need something we can call our own, something we can know to be God's will for this one person in this one time. While we do not seek a finished blueprint, we recognize that something marvelous is being revealed to us each day. A flower is unfolding, a new book is being written, an undiscovered sanctuary is being lighted a candle at a time. God is showing us who we are and what our gifts are. In this way, he is showing us his will.

We have to remember to allow ourselves to be flexible. If God is revealing his will progressively, we need to allow our lives to change progressively, as well. The accuracy of our perception of God's will might change, and we should be ready to focus our aim on a newly-perceived target. It's also true that God may have different plans for us in different stages of our lives. You may discover that God is *not* calling you to be a preacher or a doctor or whatever you thought as a freshman. Don't let this shake you up. God *is* revealing his will for you, even if it takes a while. He may first have to get rid of your own preconceptions. That may be disconcerting and it may even lead you to doubt what little you *do* know about his will, but it is the only way to the truth. Don't let it get you down.

Bill

The reason it's so impossible to give a formula for finding and following God's will is that God works individually with every person. He begins where we are in our becoming process. He can speak to us through our emotions, our thought patterns, our friends, our circumstances, or a combination of any of these. As we grow older, we probably act less and less on impulse and more and more by deliberate thought. But God can lead us in either.

Though God's leadership is an individual matter for each follower, some general guidelines may be of help to you in your search.

First, you can be pretty sure that God is not going to lead you to do something that is not consistent with his general will for all persons. He is not, for instance, leading you into an activity or occupation which is destructive to yourself or others. Though he can use *any* situation for good, God surely is not actively enlisting people into efforts which essentially do not help people in some way.

Likewise, you can be fairly certain that God is not asking you to enter or remain involved in a situation which is destructive to your own personality. This does not mean that you should withdraw from every painful or difficult situation; these can sometimes be your teachers. God often calls to hard places.

Second, God is going to continue to want you to be your most complete self. Therefore, you can be fairly sure that he will be challenging you out of your laziness and self-satisfaction. He will be wanting you to develop and use as many of your gifts as possible. Some people, given a dilemma, always conclude that God is calling them to the harder road. Each person must assess his own life at each crossroad. You probably won't always decide for the difficult path, but you probably should lean in that direction, knowing God wants continually to draw you out and help you grow.

But he wants you to be your best at whatever you do. "Whatever you are doing, put your whole heart into it," said Paul, "as if you were doing it for the Lord and not for men" (Col. 3:23, NEB).

This may mean that you will need to concentrate and really excel in certain areas, while not getting involved at all in others. One businessman keeps a pair of scissors on his desk as a constant reminder to cut our nonessentials. Building a life is constantly a matter of setting priorities and trying to keep them. You can't do everything. If you try, you will find yourself pulled apart and thinned out so you may find yourself not doing anything well.

Third, God's will for you in general is that you think primarily in terms of service rather than you own personal gain. This much is clear from the example of Jesus, who "came not to be served but to serve, and to give his life as a ransom for many" (Matt. 20:28, RSV). You may be or become wealthy and/or famous as a gift from God, but the primary meaning for your life is spiritual. This seems to be the the drift of Jesus' thought on the mountain, "Do not lay up for yourselves treasures on earth . . . but lay up . . . treasures in heaven . . . for where your treasure is, there will your heart be also" (Matt. 6:19-21, RSV).

Fourth, your attitude is all important. "Keep your heart with all vigilance," said the wise man, "for from it flow the springs of life" (Prov. 4:23, RSV). Jesus and his early followers emphasized over and over the importance of wanting to do God's will above all else—to "hunger and thirst after righteousness," to keep the eye "single," to want to do only what pleases God.

In most cases you will do well to check out big decisions with someone before you commit yourself. Talk with people who know you and will objectively evaluate your situation. Don't let anyone *tell* you what to do. You make the decision, but get some help analyzing yourself in relation to your decision. A lot depends upon knowing your gifts.

3 How Can I Discover My Gifts?

Steve

I talked about gifts in the section on knowing the will of God. To know your gift *is* to know the will of God, because he gives good gifts to be used.

Now, let's get a little more practical. A lot of courses you take as a freshman or sophomore are designed to help you discover your intellectual gifts. Don't disregard your performance in these introductory courses; it can indicate where your gifts lie and where they do *not* lie. Paying attention to grades may not seem very spiritual (Oh, to leave grades to the devil!), but God can use them to guide us. I know that "trusting the Lord" seems more like trusting your guts than trusting your grades. But if you just can't hack a subject that you *feel* you want to major in, you might as well be honest with yourself and give your guts an "F." If you don't face up to your limitations now, you'll be in for a lifelong hassle, pretending that you have gifts you don't possess.

On the other hand, you may discover a whole new area of ability, a whole new gift. That discovery can really be exciting. It can also be frustrating if you are so set in your vocational plans that the gift seems to be a diversionary tactic of the enemy. You have to accept the fact that every good gift comes from God, and you have to accept your responsibility to use that gift for God. If you discover a new gift and don't use it, you're back to the old unfaithful servant runaround, back to the eternal darkness and gnashing-of-teeth stuff. Just because you refuse to be flexible.

Discovering the gifts for relationship can be more difficult than discovering gifts for academics. You don't usually get grades for being a friend; but these gifts are just as real, and probably more important to the body of Christ. Some people are good at listening, some at teaching, some at helping out physically or financially. Some people can preach, some can give good advice, some can be affectionate.

You probably have some idea of what kind of relationships you are able to have within and without the Christian fellowship and what type of relationships seem to be the most fruitful. Think about it. Do you help others most by listening or talking, by being sympathetic or by getting tough? Different people operate in different ways, using their various gifts. It's important that we not try to be like everyone else but recognize our own unique gifts for relating to others.

Sometimes we feel most at ease in the type of relationship which is *easiest* for us. This is not necessarily the best type. We have to try to look at things objectively. What kind of relationships have really helped people grow closer to the Lord? It is often very helpful to have other Christians on campus point out your gifts to you. One of the things a group of Christian friends can strive to do is to identify one another's gifts. If that confirms your own perception of your gifts, you're more likely to start exercising your gifts. And there is always the possibility that they'll point out gifts you took completely for granted.

Bill

Paul employed the idea of gifts mainly in relationship to the church, the fellowship of believers. The principal passages on gifts are 1 Corinthians 12–14; Romans 12; Ephesians 4:1-16. Here the idea is twofold: (1) God gives spiritual gifts to be used to strengthen the church, and (2) no one is to disparage his own or another's gifts; all are needed for the group to function properly.

In New Testament times, the concept of vocation or calling in the occupational sense was not well developed. There was not much variety of occupation. Women were almost entirely confined to the home. Many of the early Christians were slaves. Being a Christian in your work was a matter of being conscientious, having a good attitude, being honest, and being a good craftsman.

The Roman Empire was not what you'd call a free society. People were not very mobile. But the church *was* a free society. The church called out people to exercise their God-given gifts. In their view this was the only way the church could be its best self.

"Now there are varieties of gifts, but the same Spirit," wrote Paul. "To each is given the manifestation of the Spirit for the common good" (1 Cor. 12:4,7, RSV). These were spiritual gifts, given to strengthen the church and its individual members. If you look at the list Paul gave in 1 Corinthians, you'll see that these spiritual gifts tend to be gifts of relationships rather than academic gifts.

The key chapters to study are 1 Corinthians 12—14. Read these openmindedly several times. Pick out the key points in the passage. Write ten sentences that summarize Paul's teaching. If you do that, I think you will come to some of these findings:

1. There is a variety of spiritual gifts.
2. Not all Christians are supposed to have the same gifts.
3. All gifts are important.
4. We are to strive for the higher gifts.
5. Genuine care for and appreciation of others is more important than the highest gift listed.
6. Speaking the gospel (prophesying) is to be desired above speaking in tongues.
7. Speaking in tongues was causing a problem in the Corinthian church, so Paul laid down guidelines to govern their use.
8. All gifts are to be used to strengthen, not destroy, the fellowship.

No one was to think his gift was unimportant; no one was to belittle another's gift. They were to relate as members of the human body—"If one member suffers, all suffer together; if one member is honored, all rejoice together" (1 Cor. 12:26, RSV).

This is a pretty high ideal, isn't it? It is difficult sometimes not to envy the brother or sister who is honored when you haven't been. It helps everyone to be a part of a church or group where the members are constantly helping one another discover and use their peculiar gifts.

Because twentieth-century America is a relatively free and mobile society, people have a good chance to work in a job which is consistent with their total gifts—their abilities, talents, dispositions, inclinations. Minority races and women sometimes find their opportunities somewhat limited, and that is deplorable.

Therefore, the Christian concept of the church can carry over into the Christian's total life. You will surely find God interested in helping you invest your life where it will do the most good.

Don't wait for an accidental discovery of your gifts. Become a part of a church, campus religious organization, Sunday School class, or some other group where honest sharing can take place.

Talk with your roommate about the significant things of your lives. All persons are searching for themselves and their place in life.

Drop by the guidance/counseling office or the campus religious activities center. Find out what tests—personality, preference, aptitude—are available. Get what help you can from them.

Try something different. Take a course that isn't a part of your curriculum. Write a poem. Learn a musical instrument. Work with a church or neighborhood children's group. See what you seem to enjoy and are good at. This should tell you some things about your gifts.

Steve: Do you really think we can talk about academic abilities as gifts? That would be a relief to me, because I have abilities in that area which are disparaged by some of the more "spiritual" Christians I know. For them, the only gifts are miraculous ones—tongues, healing, automatic prophecy, and that sort of thing. I'm not sure that your passage from 1 Corinthians can back up a broader view of gifts. What do you think, Bill?

Bill: Yes, I do think academic abilities can be thought of as spiritual gifts, though they are not included in Paul's list. The church was too young for him to conceive of all its future needs. He wasn't trying to, anyway; he only listed a few examples. Further, he was concerned about the strengthening of a struggling fellowship of believers immersed in a hostile world. His focus was not on serving the larger society.

Steve: Don't you think that this whole matter has something to do with putting down the whole secular world? Some people I know live only for those few moments when they are ecstatic and practicing their gifts. The rest of life seems to lose any significance. Can we understand gifts in a way that will give meaning to our studies and our jobs?

Bill: I continually struggle with this. In my own work I don't want to be piddling around with incidentals, but I don't believe everyone is supposed to evangelize all the time. I am coming to think of a human life as being like a many-stringed piano. We fulfill our destiny when as many of our strings as possible are in the music. Different gifts activate different strings in people. As long as our gifts help people experience the depths of their being, they seem to me to be "spiritual" gifts. Does that make any sense?

Steve: Sure. But, I'm unsure about your statement that we can carry the concept of using gifts to build up the church into our total lives. Are you saying that we ought to use our gifts to build up the world as a total whole, or that we should use all of our gifts to build up the church itself? And are gifts supposed to build up a specific church body or the "church universal"? Can we use gifts in ways that don't build up the church—both local and universal church—I believe. But, though this was not Paul's concern in this passage, our gifts should also help non-Christians. God makes rain to fall on the just and unjust (Matt. 5:45). He is interested in making life more livable for everyone.

In answer to your last question, it seems to me that if you participate in a church, you are bound to express your gifts in that church. A particular church, however, can conceivably not be ready for some of your gifts. In that case, you would have to decide whether to let part of you be dormant for awhile, use these gifts elsewhere, or join another church.

4 How Can I Know Who I Really Am?

Steve

I have to answer this question personally. Who I am may not be important to you, but it's terribly important to me. I mean, I don't stay up at night staring in the mirror in a room filled with candlelight and James Taylor, asking myself, "Who am I?" But every day I have to decide what Steve wants to do or is able to do.

If I don't know who Steve is, I'm lost. And there are times when I'm walking all alone or with the Lord and the day is so coldly quiet, when I wonder who I am and how I got to be that way. And sometimes I catch a glimpse of a figure in a dormitory mirror and I ask, "Is that really me?" And when I've been away from home for two months and I've been through some changes, I wonder if I'm quite the same person all the folks back home think I am.

When I look back on where I just came from, I realize that one Steve entered high school and another Steve left it. And when I look at myself now, I can see that the same kind of changes are going on. But what's amazing to me is the number of outside forces and circumstances that shaped me into the person I am. I wasn't born this way. I change all the time, and I don't have complete control over those changes. Do you know the feeling I'm talking about? It feels like this machine is running out of control.

It's obvious that most of the things that make up your environment are determined by somebody other than yourself. Who you are is determined more or less by powerful anonymities, and it's only rarely that you say STOP, and it's only rarely that you *can* say STOP. If you have no control over who you become, what's left but despair? You're sitting in the dorm all alone trying to be real and human and all that, and you hear the old Neil Young song, "We are helpless, helpless, helpless." And it sounds so sad and so true and maybe you want to give up because maybe only the tears are real anyway and there is nothing left but despair—unless the Lord is in control. If God is in control, everything fits together, and he is deciding who you are becoming.

That is what Paul meant when he wrote, "All things work together for good to them that love God, to them who are the called according to his purpose" (Rom. 8:28). We believe that God is all-knowing and all-powerful, so he's making all the circumstances work out for the best.

So, do outside forces take away from God? No, that's why the hollow feeling in your gut is wrong. Those forces are the hand of the Lord. Rejoice, jump up and down. All the forces of the universe are coming together to make you what you were always intended to be.

Of course it's hard to say, "It's all good" when it seems bad. You can never see Providence when you're in the middle of it, but when you look back later you know it was the Lord. I guess we come back to who *I* am, because that's what I know about and why I'm writing this anyway. A whole lot of things have happened to make me who I am. I haven't controlled where I've lived or whom I've met, but I am sure that God has used them all to make me a unique human being for his purposes. And I get "uniquer and uniquer" all the time.

Sometimes the Lord turns us around drastically. It happens a lot in college. For me, one big turnaround came in high school. I was really gungho for school activities. I was officer and actor and debater and editor of the school paper—the whole bit. There's probably nothing wrong with that, but I was putting Jesus in second place. My goal in school was not to serve the Lord, but to be president and to boost my ego. That *was* wrong. But get this: the Lord *still* used those activities to teach me things I can utilize now, for him. I was also getting to know people who were into dope and radical politics. And the Lord has used that to make me a unique part of his body, as we all are, with a unique ministry. Still, he had to shake me up.

So when I was a junior, I was suspended from school and kicked out of all activities. At that time, I almost died. All my supports had been knocked out from under me. I had to redefine who I was, so I began to turn to the Lord.

I was desperate. "Why did you let me be so stupid?" I asked God. I guess realizing my stupidity was the first step. Slowly I began to see that the Lord had his hand in the whole thing, not making me sin but allowing me to go my own way, allowing me to be punished. Now I can look back on the whole mess and say "Praise God!" Because all those nights when there was nothing to do anymore all came together for good. All those days of knowing the hurt and knowing the foolishness all came together for good, shaping me into the person God wanted me to be, drawing me closer to him. And I'm still becoming, just like you. The real trick is to praise God for the present tense, when you can't see at all how it's good. You and I both should praise God in all things, because in all things we're becoming God's unique persons.

Bill

Who you really are is related very closely to what your gifts are. Gifts have to do with *being* as well as *doing*. Each of us has areas of himself he does not know. Sometimes we fear this unknown may erupt and embarrass us or harm someone else. Sometimes it seems there's a war being fought inside. You want to be one way, but you can't somehow—this other side of you which you can't explain keeps asserting itself.

It may be of some comfort to realize that the strongest Christians of all ages have had those deep inner struggles. We have the disciples' record of two of Jesus' severe struggles with who he was and what he was to do—the temptation experience and Gethsamane, where he sweat drops of blood in his intense agony.

Paul wrote graphically, "I don't understand myself at all, for I really want to do what is right, but I can't. . . . No matter which way I turn I can't make myself do right. I want to but I can't. When I want to do good, I don't; and when I try not to do wrong, I do it anyway" (Rom. 7:15-19, TLB).

It may seem at times that your life is like an iceberg—the visible, known part is only a fraction of that which is submerged beneath the surface. The longer you live, the more of the iceberg you will likely know about; but you will never completely know yourself.

There are at least three positive ways you can react to your situation:

One is to ask for God's help. Paul cried out, "Oh, what a terrible predicament I'm in! Who will free me from my slavery to this deadly lower nature? Thank God! It has been done by Jesus Christ our Lord. He has set me free" (Rom. 7:24-25, TLB).

God is setting people free to become their best selves. He is giving us forgiveness, hope, and inner strength to face ourselves honestly and to keep getting better. The Holy Spirit makes us alive again and again. The apostle John wrote from years of being Jesus' follower: "If we say we have no sin, we are only fooling ourselves, and refusing to accept the truth. But if we confess our sins to him, he can be depended on to forgive us and *to cleanse us from every wrong*" (1 John 1:8-9, TLB). Talk to God. He is eager to hear and help.

The second way you can react to your iceberg is to explore it. Christian friends can help. Tests, reading, Bible study, prayer and meditation, group worship, work, play, and dating all help uncover the real you. Personal and group counseling and small interaction groups may be the quickest way to get to know the inner you. These experiences are often available free in a college or university. Why not investigate?

The third way you can react to your unknown is to accept yourself . . . whoever you are, whatever you may find. Try to be at home in your skin. Sure you have some strange quirks. Everyone does. You have fears and desires you don't want to have. You constantly amaze yourself because of your immature, selfish, insecure reactions.

You don't have to like these traits in yourself. Hopefully you can improve and grow where you need to. But in the meantime, don't let yourself be defeated. Talk to yourself about how you are. Shake your head at yourself. Yell! Scream! Shout! Cry! It helps. Smile if you can.

Talk to God about what you see and feel. You know God loves you and accepts you as you are. "And I am sure that God who began the good work within you will keep right on helping you grow in his grace until his task within you is finally finished on that day when Jesus Christ returns" (Phil. 1:6, TLB). You may want to memorize this verse. It is true. We may give up on·him; he never gives up on us.

I am finding it helpful also to say how I am to other people. Not just *any* others, although honest revelation can sometimes establish instant ties with perfect strangers. But little by little I am learning to tell a few others a little of how I see myself. Every person should have someone or ones to whom he can reflect his feelings, and his feelings about his feelings. Sometimes simply the naming of a fear banishes it forever. Sometimes a caring reaction can clarify or wipe out a suspicion you have about yourself.

That is why it is tremendously important to begin revealing yourself to that group or that person who can help you find yourself. If you have never begun to reveal yourself to others, it may seem like a fearful experience. But in the right setting you will discover that the more others know about you the more they will accept and love you. Cecil Osborne in *The Art of Understanding Yourself* (Zondervan, 1970, p. 22) makes this observation based on years of observing small interpersonal groups at work:

> You may never have thought of yourself as lonely, but the feeling is there just the same, unless you have broken through the barrier of your fears of rejection. And when you can reveal your true self, however slightly, you will find yourself accepted and loved at a new new level. In addition you will come to know yourself, while revealing yourself to others for our fear of being known by others is no greater than our fear of knowing ourselves.

5 How Can I Be Sure of Growing Spiritually?

Bill

Sometimes, I imagine, it seems as if you're not getting anywhere spiritually. You can't seem to quit some habit of mind or body that really bothers you. Or, you can't keep on that high plateau of attitude you want to have. Or, the trouble is you can't get *off* a plateau to be the mature person you think you should be at this point in life.

So maybe you have been wondering if you can't get on a definite program of spiritual development—like going to the spiritual YWCA—so you can be sure of growing.

The answer is probably yes . . . if you are asking the right question. Frankly, though, the question troubles me a little. Because I'm not sure but that you may be expecting not to have low spots. Like you may have the impression from somewhere that a Christian "in the will of God" or "under the leadership of the Spirit" is supposed to move through life without failure, disappointment, or sin.

Trying to live in God's purpose or will certainly helps in some ways. You don't waste as much energy, perhaps, fighting against yourself . . . or against God. You find yourself going *with* the basic intent of your life, rather than *across* it. But that doesn't mean you are exempt from problems.

At least the apostle Paul wasn't. He wrote to the Corinthian church:

We are handicapped on all sides, but we are never frustrated: we are puzzled, but never in despair. We are persecuted, but we never have to stand it alone: we may be knocked down but we are never knocked out! Every day we experience something of the death of Jesus . . . we are always facing death. . . . The outward man does indeed suffer wear and tear (2 Cor. 4:8-16, Phillips).

The apostle John wrote, "If we say that we have no sin, we deceive ourselves, and the truth is not in us" (1 John 1:8, RSV).

Apparently even the most faithful follower often finds himself in difficulty. Even Jesus, it is said, "learned obedience through what he suffered" (Heb. 5:8, RSV).

So the Christian's attempt is not to live *above* life or to be delivered *from* life, but rather to live in the *midst* of life for Jesus' sake.

Perhaps before you think further about how you can grow spiritually, you will want to decide what your goal is. You may want to get your direction before you try for distance. You probably will not see your goal as a Christian as seeing how "holy" you can be—how separated from the real world. Maybe your goal is more like seeing how much like Christ you can be . . . he gave himself for others.

The fruits of the Spirit which Paul lists in Galatians 5:22 are mostly relational: love, joy, peace, patience, kindness, goodness, faithfulness, gentleness, and self-control. It is obvious that Jesus thought his purpose in life was to help people have life and have it abundantly.

Growth into life takes both struggling and relaxing. It is both active and passive. Optimum growth for most people requires both disciplined action and creative reaction.

Because of their lack of discipline, most people accomplish in life only a fraction of what they could. Through exercising consistant effort of the right sort, most people could begin to realize a rate of growth, a development of their capabilities they never thought possible.

Take the matter of gifts we considered earlier. A few people really develop their gifts. But most seem content to make a half-hearted effort at it. Here is a good place to begin to grow. Surely

God expects us to sharpen our gifts. Too few Christians are concerned about excellence.

Prayer, Bible study, other study, Scripture memorization are other areas you may be fairly undisciplined about. Each of these opportunities for growth deserves, and must have, a thoughtful, prolonged investment of time and energy.

Bible study and prayer often go together in a growing Christian's private worship. Bible reading sometimes pinpoints an area of need or a reason for joy, which calls for prayer. On the other hand, prayer often helps a person be more receptive to God's Word, reaching him through the Bible.

One approach to Bible study is to breathe a prayer, let the Bible fall open, close your eyes, place your index finger on the page, open your eyes, and start reading.

A more systematic tack, however, is usually more profitable for most students. Use a Bible handbook, introduction, or commentary to get some background for the portion you are to study. Begin with a book which is fairly free of problems—1 John, Luke, Mark, Ephesians. Give thought and prayer to each verse. Raise questions. Pose alternate solutions to difficult passages. Make notes. Don't be too quick to run for help, but after you've puzzled awhile, read a commentary or discuss with your pastor or a close friend. Be systematic. Study the Bible daily, if only for fifteen minutes. You will be pleased with how much you learn.

Too often as children we get the impression that prayer is a couple of clichés offered at meals and a couple more at night. But prayer is actually conversing with God. You converse with a good friend at times of great happiness and great sorrow, but you also talk about other things—little and big. You share your life with each other. And there are special persons whom you'd like to know better, so you make appointments (as often as possible) to be with them.

Perhaps your friendship with God can be like that—you live in constant touch, but you also set aside time every day to be sure you get in some solid talking back and forth.

Even love, Christian love, is possibly more an art than a sentiment. You learn to love by practicing loving—by learning to do the loving action in every situation you're in. Love is a way of living. You can do a lot to improve your ability to act in loving ways toward yourself and others just by giving thought as to how to help them.

But I worry about the person who is too serious about discipline —the proper use of his time and energy—so that he is always forcing himself. Many opportunities for growth come to us serendipitously, without invitation. All day every day cannot be "programmed." A part of your Christian growth is developing sensitivity to what's happening around you—breathing deeply from the sights, sounds, smells, and sighs of life—most of all, sensing where *people* are, what's happening to those you meet.

Much of this can't be "forced," like growing a hothouse plant. It must "happen." Probably no experience in life is as growth-producing as suffering, rightly related to. No one can sympathize with a person in pain better than one who has hurt deeply himself. Yet to invite suffering is to court disaster and perhaps to tempt God. Some people say they learn more from failure than success. But a sane person doesn't deliberately "fail" so he can learn.

On the other hand, if you follow Jesus' example, you can't be overly concerned about playing safe. A step of faith may put you in physical danger, or may seem to stretch you beyond your limits. Yet a situation in which you are "over your head" may be your best chance to find out something about yourself . . . and about God. Paul said, "For therein is the righteousness of God revealed from faith to faith" (Rom. 1:17). As you follow God in faith, you learn about God and his goodness.

But there are no rules for living with God on the frontier of life. Prayer, study, developing your gifts, helping others, being open to life, and suffering are all a part of growth. You will need more of some ingredients than others to be what God wants you to be. No one but you can know what his Spirit is leading you to do.

Steve: I believe you're on the right track, Bill, but I think that when most people talk about growing spiritually they mean growing to *feel* closer to God. People say that they've grown if they've developed a greater capacity for physiological and emotional response to "religious" stimuli. There's nothing wrong with feelings, but it seems to me that for most people the period of intense feeling is relatively short-lived, only for a few months or years after a conversion or "rededication" experience. I've seen a lot of people get discouraged when the feelings fade after the peak experience. How can we avoid that kind of thing?

Bill: Have a revival twice a year? Seriously, the right kind of revivals every six months would help all of us. The problem is we don't all need the same thing to get revived, so it's not always easy to program. A person can't expect always to be on a high emotional level; emotion doesn't equal Spirit. But if we consistently seek God's leadership and do what he says, we'll be in touch with the Spirit and know that we're in touch, too.

Steve: I'd say that growing spiritually means becoming a better servant of God, which means learning obedience, not feeling. The evidence of spiritual maturity is behavior, not emotional states. Would you buy that?

Bill: Exactly.

Steve: It seems to me that as we learn to serve God, the most important trait we can develop is consistency, so that we are dependably obedient and our behavior is constantly Christian. If we learn to "keep on keeping on," we'll be able to accomplish some things for God.

6 How Can I Be Consistent?

Steve

One of the hardest qualities for a college student to achieve is consistency. You're faced with so many situations and relate to so many groups that you're likely to be a different person in different situations. Unless you've got a grasp on who you are, you'll end up being shaped by everyone around you; and you may forget who you are.

If you think it's *easy* to be yourself, just wait. You've got to work out your own beliefs and your own style, away from the stabilizing influence of home. Even as a Christian, you've got a lot to work out. When I first came to college, I was a pretty forward individual, all set to evangelize the campus. But I had to fit into the Christian community on campus, which was badly divided. I tried to be all things to all men. That didn't work too well.

The chameleon-like character of my spirituality was most evident in the way I talked. To the fundamentalists I spoke Fundese, like "the Lord Jesus Christ," "substitutionary atoning death," and other phrases I believe in but would never use; to the moderates, I spoke moderately; to the charismatics, I spoke Hallelujah-talk ("Praise God," "brother," and all that). When I was with the

Fundies, I would stand stiff with my Bible in my hand; when I was with the moderates, I would shake hands and appear intellectual; when I was with the charismatics, I would embrace. I had it down pat. But after two years or so, it began to dawn on me that I was called to be a definite somebody. I wasn't serving God by being everybody else, although I was often congratulated for being a bridge over troubled water. It's easy to be a diplomat if you have no identity. But if God made you to be a boot, to be the kicking end of his church, you'd better not try to be a stretch nylon stocking.

You may waste a lot of time in college trying to fit into everybody's mold. You have to make a deliberate effort to fight the impersonalization and manipulation that goes on even in the Christian community. Seek God's will for your own life, discover your own gifts, and act as the person God had made you. You are still a member of the community, a part of the body; but a community that limits the diversity of its parts is like a grotesque body made up of eyeballs.

Needless to say, it is no easier to maintain consistency in the non-Christian world of the campus. It is awfully easy to be a different person in the class or at parties, a person whom no one would suppose to be a Christian. There are times when it is downright embarrassing to be a Christian. A lot of us develop enormous credibility gaps, which usually seem to lie somewhere between Saturday night and Sunday morning. But becoming more and more consistent *is* what it means to grow as a Christian. Most of us have no problem attaining moments of great spirituality. The hard part is being that way all the time.

I was talking with some other students recently about spiritual maturity, trying to decide what traits they admired most in a person. Every one of them thought that the most important traits were *consistency* and *stability*. As you might guess, these were seniors talking and not freshmen. They were not concerned with being gungho or "on fire for Jesus." They were concerned with living a life of Christian witness all day every day. Each of them wanted to be someone who would not go off half-cocked, someone who would not lose his evenness of temper, someone who could always be counted on. A group of freshmen having the same discussion would probably center on zeal and activity, but I think the seniors had learned something important about the Christian life. I think God needs people who are stable and consistent. We cannot talk about growing as a Christian without talking about becoming more consistent.

Bill

The only way I know to become consistent is to try to let your every expression and action be authentic. That is, as near as possible try to take the masks off. This doesn't mean you have to be brutally frank with everyone. Temper your honesty with love. But try to quit worrying so much whether you live up to everyone's expectations. Find contentment in being yourself, however fearful or uninteresting you imagine that self to be. You will find people responding to, rejoicing in, and encouraging you in your *youness.*

7 Should I Participate in a Church?

Steve

When you get to college and you're on your own, you don't want to be distracted by the real world. You put on blinders and start singing, "The world behind me, the cross before me." Or the diploma before me, or my girl friend before me, or *anything* before me but "the world," which includes most of your Past Life and Childish Things. One of the things we want to put behind us is the church of our fathers and mothers.

Now you can put the church behind you and the cross before you if you like, but I'd rather have it the other way around. After all, the cross is an accomplished fact in the past; and the church *is* the body of our resurrected Lord in the present. If you reject the church completely, you are rejecting the resurrected Christ. As both Jesus and John Donne have said, man does not live by himself alone—which is to say, if a man thinks he lives on an island, he has probably built his house upon the sand. We really live only in relationship to others. God makes his presence known to us as we complete the circuit of his love in those relationships.

Even if you accept all of that, you still might want to drop the established church. You might say that Campus Crusade, or Intervarsity, or the Baptist Student Union are church enough for you. I'm sure you won't just shrivel up and die if you're involved in a campus fellowship. However, there is a lot to be said for plugging into an established church. Although they may be too "straight," the pastor and other leaders probably have a greater depth of maturity than students or young campus ministers. I mean, it's nice to rap with people who use the right language and who know "where you're at," "where your head's at," "what you're into," etc., etc. But every once in awhile it's going to occur to you that God works in the real world, too; and you may want to find out what's happening back there because you know that some part of you is back there, too. Right? When you've sung "Pass It On" five hundred times, a little of "Just As I Am" doesn't sound too bad. You might think, "Hey, there's a song from the country where I started this trip." And if you are especially wise, you might think, "These are my roots."

Formal worship and teaching and preaching aren't the only benefits of a church. A church keeps us in touch with the real world in a more fundamental way. By keeping us in contact with older adults, it gives us models to help us mature. By keeping us in contact with children, maybe the only children we see at school, it keeps reminding us of where we came from, reminding us to whom the kingdom belongs. The university makes children superfluous; the church makes them our hope.

We students should not, however, try to *take over* a church, either by a popular coup or by taking leadership positions that reluctant adults might otherwise fill. If we *lead* the church, we eliminate all the reasons for attending, except for fellowship. We need to serve the church, but we also have to allow the church to minister to us.

It's possible that you'll be in a college where there are no evangelical churches around. But it's not too likely. Chances are that you're being too picky about churches. You can't expect a pastor to agree with you on every point; you can't expect everyone in the congregation to be genuine or to be like you. You're not going to find a perfect church after you're out of college, and being in school doesn't give you a special right to be particular. The benefits of participating in some sort of congregation are worth the hassle.

Bill

An expression the apostle Paul uses about the church is especially apt. Among other metaphors, he refers to the church as the "body of Christ" (Eph. 1:22 f.; 4:15 f.). Christ is the head. Each Christian is an individual member of the body. Each has his own function to perform faithfully—else the whole body isn't what it should be.

Further, the members care for one another and are more than superficially related. "If one member suffers, all suffer together; if one member is honored, all rejoice together," wrote Paul (1 Cor. 12:26, RSV). The church can be, and should be, that group who can call out the best in you. It should be that warm center of support and love that all of us need.

The church is the community where faith is born, disciples are nourished, and love is learned. One can no easier be a Christian apart from the living community of Christians than a man can be born without parents or speak without a language. A solitary Christian is no Christian at all. He cannot possibly mature without bearing another's burden, or he cannot become the full man whom God meant him to be until he helps another man to become the same. The Christian situation requires that every person live in the company of other Christians, breathe common air, and be committed to one another's good. Christianity requires that we belong together and know it." (Robert Hamill, *Gods of the Campus,* Abingdon, 1949, pp. 46 f.)

The church can also help you help others. As good as your intentions may be, as lofty as your pronouncements, you may find it very difficult to get into helping others. It's often hard to go it alone. But in most churches you will find others who share your concerns; you can help one another organize and get into a continuing ministry of some sort. The church may already have work going that you can become a part of.

Money is sometimes an unpopular subject, and I wouldn't bring it up . . . except that maybe one of the most important opportunities a church offers you is to help others around the world—many others . . . whom you can never see or know . . . and who can never thank you.

Join a church with the idea of being a participating member. Sing in the choir, attend Sunday night worship, work with children/youth. Get to know other members.

And don't overlook the fellowship to be found in campus religious organizations like the Newman Club and Baptist Student Union. These Christian students are members of the body of Christ, too.

8 How Can I Deal with Problems in the Christian Community?

Steve

We live our Christian lives in community, and the condition of our community is often the measure or the cause of our own spiritual condition. But the community of Christians on any campus is heir to all the weaknesses and divisions of the church universal, in spite of the apparent similarities of students. A lot of times we just don't get along. This is hard to explain to non-Christians, and it should be even harder to explain to God; but on many campuses different groups of Christians are at one another's throats. What a show, says the non-Christian, staring in amazement, in desperation.

We need to recognize the absurdity of our struggles, but the question here is "How can I deal with them?" Well, you can't. Not by yourself. These are community problems, and they must be dealt with by the community. To name yourself Crusader and Forger of Union is to fall prey to the same sort of individualism and egotism that causes divisions in the first place. You do a lot better to instill in the Christians on campus a sense of themselves as a community, a self-consciousness as the body of Christ. What the body needs is not little Kissingers but little Christs; not diplomatic finessers but great lovers.

Our first task in dealing with these problems is not getting groups together, but getting ourselves together. My own attitude toward divisions will affect my witness more than the fact of the divisions themselves. Some students become so obsessed and agonized over conflicts between groups that it ruins their relationships with individuals. That doesn't help anything. Every individual Christian is a member of the body of Christ, and I can be one with him as an individual even if our groups are officially at war. And we need to see that divisions are not bad in themselves. God wants diversity in his church, and it is normal for groups to split and grow by splitting. The problems come when there is strife and envy among groups.

Problems often arise when several groups are competing for the loyalties of the same group of students. If there are no clear-cut criteria, such as denominational background, for sorting students into various groups, group loyalties tend to center around personalities and style. Certainly there is room for different styles or worship, ministry, and fellowship; but each group ought to consider whether its function is useful to the body of Christ on campus. There is probably no need for several groups to carry out identical ministries while other ministries are neglected.

When competition among Christian groups arises, some groups often try to beat out the competition by being the most exclusive and by touting themselves as spiritually superior. This kind of collective ego-tripping is not limited to one kind of Christian group; I've seen it in fundamentalists, liberals, charismatics—in any group that makes one element of doctrine or practice more important than the person of Christ and his body.

Christians on my campus have been divided into less-than-friendly groups for many years. Some groups condemn others as "apostate" or "fanatic." One group warns freshmen to stay away from other groups; they have even confronted members who participate in other ministries, warning them that they are falling away, becoming "unequally yoked." Some of us can't understand. "We are one body," we say. "Can't we love one another?" But the dividers say, "The Word is the word." What they are really saying is, "I would rather be right than be loving." What they say to outsiders is, "I have never known love." It's hard to take. They might as well rip out my heart with their bare hands. For if they have never known oneness with other Christians, if they have never known love, we are not talking about the same Jesus. I know nothing of a separated Jesus.

I suppose I exaggerate the trauma. But I do want to say that this sort of division can undermine your own faith because it calls into question your personal knowledge of Jesus by casting the Christ-life in a new, harsher light. While I want to emphasize the centrality of community in the Christian life, I can't be dependent on that community for life itself. Our life comes from the person Christ himself, and the failure of the community—although weakening our faith and witness—does not cut off our relationship to Christ.

It is when you as a freshman first choose a group that divisions are brought home. Obviously, you have to pray about the choice. But the decision ought to be based on moral grounds, biblical grounds, more than on the basis of "warm feelings." You can't join a Christian fellowship like a fraternity, picking the elitist group because you get a bid. Sometimes the group that has the closest fellowship is growing the least. Some freshmen say, "I think I'll join Group X because it is the closest, most tight-knit fellowship." That's a pretty dubious reason, especially if that closeness stems from the very fact of exclusiveness and self-congratulation. If closeness stems from a rejection of outsiders, it is immoral; and it is immoral for you to enjoy that closeness. I mean, the Mafia is tight-knit. Right? When you pick a group, try to decide where God can best use your gifts, which is where you can grow.

Bill

All this may sound a bit negative, like, Why should I worry about these Christian communities if they're all at one another's throats? Why not let them die a natural death?

Don't let us frighten you off. We're just trying to be realistic. The good of these fellowships far outweighs the bad. Every Christian

40

on campus really needs a group, imperfect as it is bound to be.

Actually, the situation varies a good bit from campus to campus. On a large state-supported campus where several denominational and/ or nondenominational organizations are fairly well established and where the students are legion, each campus religious group tends to be rather a community unto itself.

Baptist Student Union alone at a medium-sized school in East Texas, for instance, probably reaches a thousand students during the year in Bible studies, choirs, and mission activities. Other religious groups on campus are also busy. While you may be aware of the presence of other groups and may have some joint concerns and projects, you will probably do well to have real community with the members of your own group.

In a situation like this, you doubtless will find yourself trying to decide whether to join a group which is already pretty well organized and in which you probably won't exert much influence for a year or so. You will have time to observe, participate, and have your own needs ministered to for awhile before big responsibilities for the group are laid on you.

You might find this is the case if you attend a church-related school, particularly of your own denomination. Religion may seem to be everywhere, and your participation may be largely of an observer nature at first. The upperclassmen likely will have the leadership positions—as it should be.

In these two preceding conditions, you may see your choices as between different activities within the same group rather than choosing among groups.

On many campuses, as Steve, implied, you may find yourself sooner or later a part of a rather small group which is really serious about being Christian. You may have heavy burdens laid on you for what seems like the major Christian witness on campus. If you survive, this is where you may grow the most. One reason: it's more obvious that you need God to help you.

Whatever your campus makeup, however, it will help your perspective to remember that your group is only a *part* of the body of

Christ. God has other followers, some of whom you know not. Each group has its contribution to make to his kingdom.

Steve: Thanks for coming back like that, Bill. I have to admit that I was writing a lot more about Princeton than about the average college campus. We have a relatively small group of active Christians in several groups which have to compete for the small group of active Christian freshmen. I don't want to get everybody all shook up about problems.

Bill: You are being realistic; but I tend to get uneasy, I guess, when those campus groups (which I work with all the time) come off sounding shaky.

Steve: And even with all the problems, my experiences in the Christian groups at Princeton have been fantastic. They are the experiences that will always mean the most to me.

Bill: Confronting real problems usually is not pleasant. That's why most of us would rather avoid them. Getting involved has long-term values that can't be appreciated or measured at the time.

9 How Can I Relate to Christians of Different Religious Orientation?

Steve

A campus fellowship is always a mixed bag, and you never know what kind of Christian is going to grab you next. It's easier to deal with people who are different from you if you think of them as groups or as ideologies. But the time comes when you are called to relate to them as individuals.

Picture this scene: You're walking around campus to your room, and there's that guy on the street corner again, handing out tracts. You know, the one with the motorcycle jacket with stitching on the back: "King Jesus Is Coming." You don't really want to talk to him, but he has you sized up. Stepping into your path, breathing in your face, handing you a pamphlet (it's the one for dopers, you can tell by the psychedelic colors), he asks, "Are you saved?" It seems the easiest thing, so you just say, "Yes. Praise the Lord. Good-bye." But when you get back in your room alone and lie on your bed, when you start to think about it, it's not so easy. You think, "I know the answer to that question, but I'm not sure he understands the question. I'm not sure that he believes my answer or that I'd believe his."

Then the Lord comes to you and an image of that guy on the street corner comes to you, and there is a voice: "This is your brother;

43

you are hand and foot of the same body, moving together, bleeding into each other, not knowing." And the image of that guy stands in absolute darkness, breathing hard just to keep shining, looking for another light.

The next day there he sits in the student center, alone. You, it's time. Sit down next to him. "Howdy, my name is _____," you say. "I'm a Christian, too. How has it been going?" Maybe he'll tell you that like wow, you're the first Christian he's met on campus, praise God. Maybe you'll ask if he's heard of this fellowship and that group, and he'll say, "You're kidding. That many Christians?" Maybe you can learn what *brotherhood* means.

Or, rewrite the script. (Scene: Student Center) "Hallelujah," he says, putting his greasy hand on your shoulder. "Have you been baptized in the Spirit?" "Well," you say. "Let me tell you about that. . . ."

Or, rewrite. "Hey, man," he says, lifting his heavy Scofield off the table. "You're not in that liberal BSU, are you? I'd rather spend my time in the Word." "Well," you say, choking on your coffee. . . .

Chuck that, you're thinking, or chalk it up to experience. But you can't just do that. You don't agree about everything—so what? You've still met a brother in Christ, you are still one with him, and you are still called to develop your relationship with him. God did not bring you together in this place for no reason. It may not be easy to get close, but if you can just catch his eye, if you just look into his eyes with love as long as he will let you, you can communicate more of oneness nonverbally than you could convey in hours of doctrinal debate. Find out where he's at with regard to his studies, his family, romance, hamburgers, and all those things that matter to human beings. If you try to build a relationship between two different persons instead of between two different ideologies, you can learn to love.

Of course, there is a certain element of risk involved here. It's a lot easier to stick with people exactly like yourself, and it's easier to choose not to change. Differences with Christian friends may cause you more interior hassles than trying to convert the heathen, especially if the differences concern central questions: the object and

44

content of faith; the relationship of faith, reason, and the revealed word; the method of salvation; the functions of the Trinity. You have to remember that these are not easy questions with obvious answers which others simply overlook. They have been very hard questions for at least nineteen centuries. Nevertheless, you have to find the best answers you can, and live by them.

When your friends settle on different answers which disagree with yours, this sets up contradictory reactions which may be hard to handle. On the one hand, you feel that these are brothers and sisters whom you ought to trust; and you want to agree with them if only for the sake of unity. On the other hand, you know that the truth is the truth, and you feel that if these people don't have an adequate conception of salvation, they may not even be true Christians. Both of these responses arise from good impulses, but they create a tension inside you. You may try to get rid of this tension by throwing yourself on one side or another. But to throw yourself on the side of passive acceptance may mean believing lies, and to give yourself a monopoly on the truth is in itself a lie. I've found that this tension is the only healthy state, that it is a condition found in all growing Christians facing new ideas. This tension enables you to learn from other people and still remain willing to share the truth with them.

Bill

If you read between the lines of Paul's first letter to the Corinthian church, especially 1 Corinthians 12—14, you see that this early church was full of disagreements about some pretty basic stuff. In the midst of his discussion of spiritual gifts in this passage, Paul inserted 1 Corinthians 13, insisting that *love* was the most important Christian trait. Perhaps it is typical that a serious divisive controversy brought forth three of the most significant chapters in the entire Bible.

The truth is that most of the New Testament books were written as letters to churches which were having problems. Even the four Gospels were likely written to support particular views or to counteract fallacious teachings by professing "Christians."

Good often comes from conflict. It has a better chance if the two conflictees love each other and if each can listen to what the other is saying. To be open is to continually experience the stimulation of new ideas—a very desirable state. This openness needs to be balanced, however, by analytical thinking.

Analytical thinking is both a trait and a discipline. Some people seem naturally to be able to cut away emotion and excess verbiage and get right to the heart of an issue. Computerlike, they are able to compare present information they are receiving to data stored in their brain recesses. Their recall is often astounding.

Doubtless some have received this trait in part as a gift. But countless others have *learned* to think analytically. They have systematically developed their thinking mechanism and fed it nutritional information. When new "facts" come in, they can compare them, because they have something stored. Further, they learn to separate a person from his ideas. They can question or even attack an idea without malice toward the person who holds it. They refuse to allow themselves or their friends to get by with sloppy reasoning.

I have a good friend (incidentally, a physics professor) who is very disconcerting. He thinks about what you say. If it doesn't "click" with his own set of data, he lets you know. It took awhile for me to begin to learn that Joe was not out to put me down. It is just that Joe's mental makeup isn't compatible with sloppy thoughts.

It's good to have friends like Joe. Each of us probably needs to be that kind of friend more often. To be questioned or to question is sometimes painful, but it eventually yields a very valuable result. For some months now, I have been trying to raise the questions that bother me, rather than let statements roll by on tacit agreement. I sometimes feel I am deliberately trying to undermine a person; often I have to be sure I'm not. But in the process I'm finding I'm helping to clarify communication, to find out more from the speaker, and to better assemble my own thoughts. I'm getting to where I don't even fear being thought stupid.

The question is a very valuable resource when you are in a conflict of ideas. It shouldn't be used as a manipulative gimmick; but an honest, probing question can give both you and your "adversary" time to think. It sometimes can change the direction of a conversation or make a point much less abrasively than a direct statement.

Another valuable resource is correct information. The facts have ruined a lot of good arguments. Read the Bible and books about the Bible regularly. Do your own topical Bible studies in areas where you seem to be in conflict with your fellow Christians. Get a concordance and look up all the passages on speaking in tongues, for instance. Summarize each passage in a sentence or two. Put these together into Your Very Own Biblical View of this matter. Then read a book or two on the subject, but not like a sponge. Compare the author's views to Your Very Own Biblical View. Where do you need to give? Where does the author? Share your insights and questions in discussions with your friends who are charismatics.

You are going to run into all sorts of new ideas about God from professors and students. Each of these needs biblical perspective applied.

One of the most "openminded" views on campus is that God is not a person. Instead, he is "truth" or "love" or some other generic concept or value. The person who holds this view may do so to avoid oversentimentalizing God. He may have some pretty valid criticisms to make of traditional Christians. If you happen to encounter him, find out what he believes and why. Ask questions. Listen carefully. In the meantime, do Your Very Own Biblical View of this by reading in the New Testament and noting references to God. Is there room in Paul's thought for a nonpersonal God?

Whatever your encounters may be, go forth with these three yeoman resources: an open mind, an honest question, and a search for facts.

10 How Can I Witness Without Turning People Off?

Steve

When it comes to witnessing, there are different strokes for different folks. By "witnessing," I mean giving explicit testimony to Jesus Christ. By "folks," I mean both the witnessers and the witnesses. Different Christian folks should have distinctive styles of witness, and those styles of witness should vary with the different non-Christian folks toward whom the witness is directed.

A campus is a crazy place; and witnessing can get crazy, too. You know what it's like: getting run down by an elephant with "One Way" painted on his side, baptizing with his trunk. Or maybe just seeing a Jesus-mouse squeaking alone at the behemoth university. Some people want to give Haircuts for Christ; some want to give Orgies for the Lord. A lot of places you can't sit down on a toilet anymore without seeing a Bible verse scrawled on the wall.

Now, that's a lot of witnessing—and maybe that's good. But there comes a time when we have to consider the question of effectiveness. If we are really witnessing in order to help people to know God and not just to make ourselves feel good or look good, effectiveness should be a central concern. It should worry us when we turn people off. Of course, some people will reject the gospel; and, of course, we have to depend on the Holy Spirit. But we need to be sure that what people are rejecting is the gospel and not our own personalities. Some Christians take a perverse delight in being obnoxious in witnessing, feeling that the more they are rejected the holier they are. This is sin. If you cause someone to reject the gospel because you are on an obnoxious ego-trip, you're going to be held accountable.

You can't bear true testimony to the true Lord if you're not completely honest and genuine and living. A fake testimony kills. Impersonality kills. This is as true when you're giving a witness to Christians as when you're sharing the gospel for the first time.

You must have met some of those people—the ones with eyes that nail you to the wall and sweet smiles that never fade away. You must have been sitting alone sometime thinking of lost friends and times gone by and the damage done; thinking, *Oh, momma, momma, I wish I knew how to cry.* And one of them sits and smiles and tells you not to worry and to trust the Lord, and isn't Jesus living in you? And you think, *Jesus, I wish he knew how to cry.* And you say, halting, "Brother, I have a problem." He smiles and praises God, telling you about his carefree life in Christ. Your eyes are melting, saying, *Brother, I have a hurt*; but his eyes never change. Your eyes are closing, saying, *Brother, have you never known the hurt, Brother, have you never known that Jesus wept, Brother, just touch my hand, please.* And he is so calm, reading, "I am crucified with Christ. . . ."

Do you see what I am trying to say about witnessing? Have you ever been hurt by someone who refused to listen to you, who chose not to be personal, who gave you a prefab spiel rather than relationship? Your non-Christian friends may react to you the way you react to this ever-smiling evangelist, or to the guy on the corner handing out tracts. They may have no idea of what you are trying to communicate if you speak on no level deeper than the canned-jargon level. They want to hear from your heart, in your heart's own language. That will be, after all, the language that speaks to *their* hearts.

There's a lot of difference between an impersonal witness and a personal relationship. If you're not willing to establish a relationship with the person you're talking to, they might as well talk to a tract or a TV show or a Bible. God chooses to use you, a person, because God works in relationships. His love is made perfect in our love for others, and it is in that love that the non-Christian sees God most clearly.

In trying to share yourself, as well as the message of the gospel, you've got to be yourself. You've got to have your own natural style. If you mimic the styles of other Christians, all you'll be able to share of yourself is that mask. You have to be honest and open to questions. But in responding to questions, you have to be careful where you draw the battle lines; don't draw them over territory not worth defending. Don't draw the line at evolution or Cain's wife or the Flood. Center on central issues: man's need for salvation, and God's fulfillment of that need in Christ. To say that you're not settled on one of the side issues is not the same as yielding to the point. It allows you to move on to the question of relationship to God.

Bill

For many Christians, witnessing is another one of those points of tension between *is* and *ought to be.* I still remember vividly (over several years now) my attitude toward witnessing when I was in college. The idea of talking with somebody about becoming a Christian terrified me. I tried to avoid even the thought of it. I was glad to preach in revivals, work in missions, be responsible for worship services, and many other things. But I steered clear of "soul winning," as church people called it. I gave wide berth to the room at church where they had "soul-winning training." I kept being afraid someone would reach out and pull me in.

In part, this fear was doubtless due to a misunderstanding of what witnessing is. Though I had often heard the term, I just had never been able to see myself as a soul winner. Some gaps had been in my earlier church experience, and somehow I had always managed to escape verbal witnessing efforts. The ideas was strange to me.

But I think I also avoided witnessing because I feared, deep down, that I didn't have what I was supposed to be sharing with others. I had real difficulty experiencing the exhuberance that a friend of mine had, for instance. I kept trying to find this missing "something."

I could discuss religion with people; I often did with my room-mates and fraternity brothers. I invited people to church. I'm sure I tried at times to make some sort of case for church or God or even Christ. But it all seemed rather dry and academic—a kind of matching of wits . . . which I didn't feel I could win. I had no aliveness to share that seemed different from what everyone else had.

But my attitude toward witnessing changed dramatically within the first year after graduation from college. Witnessing was not the central issue of the change, though evangelism was involved.

As a single, 21-year-old electrical engineer, I was still very much of a part of the "youth set" at First Baptist Church, Chattanooga, Tennessee, when a city-wide youth-led revival began to come to town. I was asked to take a major responsibility for the revival preparations and activities, which I accepted in my accustomed manner (having usually been asked at some time to be president of all the religious organizations I'd ever joined).

But this revival responsibility turned out to be different. I had been sailing along, rather perfunctorally going through the motions of leadership. At Saturday night prayer meeting before the revival was to begin on Sunday, the seriousness of this event and my part in it began to dawn on me. I was in charge of the prayer meeting, so I was going to close the "sentence" prayers of the rather small group of young people who were involved to this point. The more people prayed, the more I realized I probably needed help worse than anybody—not just for myself, but for the usefulness of the revival.

When it came to me to pray, I confessed my need of God and determined as best I could to put him first in my life that week. Somehow, the prayer and the situation affected me at a very significant level. As the week progressed, I began to have a freedom, a joy, an ease in doing religious things I had never experienced before. I found myself wanting more than anything in the world to follow God's lead in every area of my life, to be his completely.

During and immediately following the week I noticed some

perceptible changes in my behavior, some of which I still remember. One, I was able to quit smoking cigarettes rather easily, after having struggled to quit for a couple of years without success. Also, the Bible began to make sense to me, even some of Paul's difficult letters in the King James; and I began to enjoy—really enjoy—reading it.

Further, my "joy" continued. I found myself (1) wanting to be with other Christians a lot, and (2) wanting to tell other people how I thought they might find this great happiness in God which had come upon me. And I began to try to tell them. One by one, and in small groups, I cornered my colleagues at the office, the guys at the National Guard, and other people I knew. Mine was not a sinister plan designed to catch an adversary unaware and snare him. It was a rather naive, uncomplicated, straightforward checkup with my friends to see if they were participating in this abundant life. I couldn't believe that even many of those who were professing Christians were really having this joy, because they had never said anything about it and church didn't seem to be very important to them.

Then I discovered that my times of greatest inner peace and sense of doing God's will were when I was talking with people about God and Jesus. At first I thought I had to "feel" an overwhelming joy at the moment, else I couldn't witness to someone. But as the ups and downs of life came, I found that this was wrong. I realized that I was in touch with a Reality that had meaning for all experiences.

Since those early days of beginning to "witness," without really calling it that, I have come to some rather firm convictions about it.

First, the Holy Spirit is he who works with people's minds/hearts to open them to change in response to a Christian's witness. He can use both the most polished and the most halting testimony. Sometimes he seems to specialize in using unlikely circumstances to touch a person's life. He can help us know the right words to say. He can guide us in our actions.

Second, our witness can be much more spontaneous and heartfelt if we have ourselves experienced and are continuing to experience the uplifting presence of God.

Third, every Christian should, as a part of his way of life, be talking about his own experience with God and be helping others to relate more meaningfully to God. Generally, it seems the more we think about sharing, and try to share, the more opportunities we have.

Fourth, no two people are exactly alike. In general, the better we know a person, the easier it will be for the Holy Spirit to lead us to say/do the best thing for him. There is always the possibility, however, that a chance encounter or a short visit may uncover a spiritual need that God can fill immediately. Sometimes strangers get to the heart of things more quickly than friends.

Fifth, God can use each of us as we are now. You can reach someone that no one else can. Of course, you can improve and grow—you can know more and learn to explain better—but God can use your particular set of traits if you'll let him. You don't have to become like someone else.

We have to be careful comparing our "success" in witnessing with someone else's. A lot depends on our gifts and on where we find ourselves. William Carey, the first English missionary to the Orient, worked and witnessed several years before he saw the first convert to Christianity, but he really laid the foundation for all subsequent foreign mission effort.

Sixth, "witnessing" and "winning" are two different things. See No. 1 above.

One of the tensions in witnessing for many Christians comes at the point of "style" or "approach." In a way, it seems foolish to talk about developing a "style of witnessing," even if it's "your own" style. If you are different from everyone else, and if each person you meet is a unique individual with his own background, attitudes, and needs, how can you develop a style which fits all situations? Can't the Spirit lead you as you are to say/do the best thing for the other person as he is?

Theoretically, yes. And that is the sort of goal every Christian should work toward.

As you read the Gospel accounts of the life of Christ, you probably are not aware of any emphasis Jesus gives to a certain "style" or approach to witnessing.

To religious leader Nicodemus, he spoke of the need for a radical reorientation (new birth) toward God, not just a minor adjustment in ritual.

To a woman coming to draw water, he spoke of the well of living water springing up into eternal life.

To shepherds and farmers, he spoke of sheep and bread and grain and weeds and lilies of the field.

Yet, he wasn't always direct and plain. Sometimes he used parables, sometimes other subtle means to cause people to think and to avoid falling into the common understanding of the nature of God.

It is a beautiful thing when your perception can be so accurate and your witness so naturally on target that the person is obviously helped . . . and you didn't even have to try remembering the ABC's of the gospel.

Generally, however, communication is not that perfect or natural. Some persons either don't know or don't reveal what's really bothering them. If you respond to every question a person asks, you may spend a lot of time "chasing rabbits" and helping the person avoid the confrontation he really needs. Your "style" of witness is basically consistent with your personality—it is going to reflect your own uniqueness as a person—as it should. If you are aggressive and controlling as a person, your witness will likely tend to be direct and forceful. If you are more passive and retiring, your witness will naturally tend to take on these characteristics.

Only for the sake of the gospel and other people, you probably won't be able to let your witness be "what just comes out." As you would develop any other communication or relational skill, you will doubtless need to keep working on your verbal witnessing. You need to confront people more directly if you are too passive. If your approach is "canned" and always the same, you need to work at responding better to individual persons. If you find yourself casting a warm influence but never getting to the point, you need to structure yourself more.

In any case, you should have in mind (or in your New Testament or on a pamphlet or on a "cheat sheet") a clear, biblical answer to certain obvious questions. What is a Christian? Why become a Christian? How does one become a Christian? It will probably help at first to have a definite outline of how you would answer these questions. As you can, you should develop biblical and logical answers to the more common questions people raise about being a Christian.

There is really no valid reason why a Christian can't be both supersensitive to a person's individual desires and needs and also skilled in helping him open up to God. Yet this is one of the areas where many Christians fail to develop themselves. No one can prescribe what your particular "style" should be. You should be sharing the good news in the best way possible. You have the example and words of others, the witness of the Bible, the corrective influence of the church, and the internal leadership of the Spirit to help you grow.

But you will probably always feel a healthy tension toward doing better. I hope so.

Another related tension some people experience about witnessing is, How much time should I spend at it?

Your main job is being a student. Common sense and the leading of the Lord to get you this far would indicate you should do a good academic job. This would seem to mean you should set some sort of limit on the number of minutes or hours per week you spend talking with people about religion. On the other hand, you can reason, with merit, "How can any of this history, English, or math be as important as another person's relationship to God? How can my study for this test tomorrow be as vital as talking to my roommate tonight?"

College students have resolved this dilemma in a myriad of ways. Some have concluded they should concentrate on their studies and catch up on religion when they graduate. Others have limited their witnessing to natural encounters with friends, family, and classmates. Others have scheduled a definite time each week to visit students whom they think are unbelievers. Still others major on witnessing, particularly at certain times, trusting in God to help them on tests, term papers, and other academic activities.

This is another tension I believe you'll have to live with. You'll have to make your own decision. If you tend not to be studious, you'll probably need to build yourself some fences around your religious activities, including personal witnessing. I believe God helps us on both intake and recall. But I also believe learning goes a lot deeper than getting past the next exam.

You will probably find yourself doing better at witnessing and everything else if you set us some sort of time budget. Make it flexible so that you can decide to alter the balance for special events like campus revivals and final exams. But make time each week to initiate religious conversations with people. If some of these conversations come to you by chance, work on making these natural relationships as meaningful as possible. But don't wait. Listen to people. Check religious preference lists. Notice habits. Pray. Seek out someone who may be hurting inside.

11 How Can I Relate to Christians with Different Styles of Witness?

Steve

This is basically the same problem as relating to Christians of different orientations, but maybe we can get more specific in the context of witnessing. Differences in witnessing style are often the surfaces of our spiritual lives which rub each other the wrong way because witnessing is often where our theology of salvation is most obvious in practice.

It would be easy for us to dismiss these differences in approach as really insignificant, but we would be avoiding the basic problem. The problem is learning to accept diversity in the body of Christ. Differences of style often stem from differences in emphasis in our understanding of grace, but we have to learn to live as part of a body in which there are always different parts with different emphases.

Let's look at two messed-up concepts of salvation that have a profound effect on witnessing. They're probably the oldest heresies around, and I find myself slipping into one or the other pretty often.

The first is the old "salvation through works" trick. A lot of us just don't believe, deep down, that salvation is by grace and not by being good. This kind of "salvation" only leads to neurosis. It makes you worry all the time that you're not doing well enough or just not doing enough. Then if you try to witness, you're like an uptight sales-man at the door, saying, "Sir, I've got this great stuff that's being given away, only, I'm not sure I've got it yet, and you'll have to work yourself to death in order to get it, but it's really hot stuff and it's free, even though, uh . . . ." Not too many takers on that one. A lack of assurance about salvation naturally produces a lack of assur-ance about witnessing. The way to relate to a Christian friend who's extremely hesitant about sharing his faith is not to attack his style or his personality. You need to help him, gently, to a fuller understand-ing of grace. Encourage him, since it is his insecurity that makes him hesitant. The easiness with which you talk about your faith may help him along, and the completeness with which *you accept him* will help him to understand how completely *God accepts him.*

The second problem is believing you're so saved that you don't have to worry about *anything.* I've had guys tell me (honest), "Hal-lelujah, brother, Jesus lives in me and I *can't* sin." Now that may be a nice feeling, but salvation just doesn't work that way. This is just an ego-trip charged to Jesus. This type of hyped-up "spirituality" can make a witness unbearably arrogant. It's like a salesman who barges in with a vaudeville band. "Hey! Just look at me, brother—*Me* with a capital "M" and that rhymes with Him and that's who you need; fol-low my lead (ta-dum) and be (ta-dum) just (boom) ME! (Rooty-tooty-ooty-oop!)"

There are two probable reactions to this type of pitch. Some people will say, "I don't care if it *is* free. I don't want to be an arro-gant pig like you." Others will say, "Wow, you're so great, I could never be like you; I could never be a Christian." Either way, you lose and they lose.

As a normal red-blooded Christian, your response to a person with this sort of witnessing style will probably be something like, "Well, look, brother, if you think you don't have any sins, let me point them out: No. 1 . . . ." But that's not quite the best way to build a relationship with that person. Besides, he's operating in a closed system in which he can say that anyone who hasn't seen the spiritual light shouldn't be listened to. He may say that you're just projecting your own sins onto him.

Your response to this person should be like your response to any person—a response of honesty and love. Your being honest with him and confessing your problems can do more than anything else to open him up. And if he feels secure in your love for him, he can feel free eventually to admit that he is human and troubled. Of course, you don't want to give approval to his ego-trip. There is room for suggestion, such as, "Brother, I talked to Sally Sinner today, and I think you may be scaring her away from the Lord. Don't hassle her too much, OK?" But such suggestions have to be made gently, and you can't expect him to go along. Anticipate the reaction: "Oh, she's being convicted." Point out that she may just be turned off by him, but make it clear that you're not.

These caricatures are not meant to imply that every witness should strive for the Golden Mean, or the Golden Nice. There is a lot of room for diversity in styles of witness within the campus community. We need some people who speak out articulately, some who show excitement, and some who know how to listen. Each kind of witness should recognize that the other kinds are important; there is a cumulative effect in the witness of the whole community. If the non-Christian sees love and oneness among the members of that community, he will interpret this witness as a balanced whole. If he sees Christians as fragmented, he will interpret their several witnesses as incomplete entities.

This is why it is crucial that we have cooperation in witnessing rather than competition. The different parts of the body do not act alike, but they act together. When we are embarrassed by another Christian's witness or lack of witness, we must not take the easy path of dissociating ourselves, saying, "Oh, him, he's a fanatic. That's not what a Christian is. Listen to what *I* say." Rather, we should be saying, "We are different parts of one body. You have to look at us as a whole to see how God works."

Bill: Your point, Steve, about differences in style being based on differences in theology seems valid. I had never really thought in these terms. I think of differences in witnessing style more in terms of how structured the approach is. Most of the students I've encountered who are interested in witnessing seem to have similar theology. But either because they differ in the way they see others or in their own need for structure, these students vary a lot on the passive-aggressive scale.

Steve: I'll agree that most witnessing students have a similar theology, but I was thinking of the broader spectrum of Christian students. We could think of *not* witnessing, that is, keeping quiet as a "style of witness." I see that most variation in style among witnesses is in terms of passiveness and aggressiveness. I think the most predominant style of witness is "silent witness." That style may have a lot to do with personal theology.

Bill: True. Some of the silent witnesses undoubtedly grew up in a church environment that did not emphasize person-to-person, verbal evangelism. In fact, some religious traditions in their current expression may be reacting against a historical enthusiasm or revivalism. They guard themselves against any sort of "instant evangelism," believing that lasting evangelism comes through growing up in and with the church—experiencing education, worship, the "sacraments," and so forth.

On a more personal level, however, I believe a lot of Christian students don't witness because nothing spiritually significant has really happened to them—nothing they can identify, anyway. This really is *personal* theology.

Steve: Of course a genuine witness has to grow out of a personal relationship with God, but I wouldn't want to ignore differences in witnessing that are strictly personal and not theological. I mean, some people grow up to be shy, and some grow up to be brash. A lot of witnessing style comes from personality, and we ought to take that personality into account. Just because someone is shy, we don't have to say he has lousy theology. I seem to be undermining my own point here, but I don't want you to go overboard. Witnessing style shouldn't be set up as a barometer for theology.

Bill: I think personality differences among Christians are extremely important. They say something about both how and to whom a person can witness most effectively. Undoubtedly these differences come from both religious background and all other factors that have fashioned the person.

Steve: Bill, you probably know more about other denominations. Don't you think that different church backgrounds could make a big difference in the way a person witnesses?

Bill: Some religious traditions emphasize church membership, rather than personal relationship with God, as the essence of salvation. This emphasis is based on the belief (theology) that salvation is in the church. A Christian who grew up in this tradition would have difficulty in seeing the importance of a "personal decision to follow Christ" apart from "joining the church and following its teachings." The two ideas are the same to him. The Holy Spirit does not lead him apart from what the church teaches and has taught.

Some other traditions believe that a person is led by the Holy Spirit only through the words of the Bible—the Holy Spirit has no relationship as person to person.

Steve: But you don't really agree with these two view points, do you?

Bill: No, I'd emphasize a personal relationship to God.

Steve: Just checking. Anyway, you see we're getting back to my original point about the relationship of personal theology and witnessing style. I guess it's mostly a matter of what you believe about salvation, right? Like believing in salvation through works or the church, or believing in super-salvation from all sin.

Bill: A Christian's belief about salvation is critical for understanding student response to the gospel, as well as for building a basis for his witness. Perhaps it would help to think about the meaning of salvation.

Bill

Some student indifference and hostility is because of the nature of the Christian gospel itself. Salvation has never seemed either reasonable or necessary except to one who recognizes his own deep need. The apostle Paul spoke accurately for all times and places when he wrote to the Corinthian Christians that the "word of the cross is folly to them who are perishing . . . a stumbling-block to Jews and folly to Gentiles" (1 Cor. 1:18-25, RSV). "Where is the wise man? . . . the scribe? . . . the debater?" Paul asks. God does not save by wisdom but by the "foolishness" of the gospel, he asserts.

In fact, it often seems that too much reasoning hinders a person from the radical capitulation that being a Christian believer demands.

Burnett was an intelligent liberal arts student in a small private college in Tennessee. He had grown up in a church and become a member and "believer" as a young teen-ager. He did a lot of thinking about religion during college years, never completely dropping out of the church. But by his senior year he was classifying himself as an agnostic. He was hung up on his own indecision. He couldn't relax and grow as a Christian because he wasn't sure that God was real; yet he couldn't turn his back on the possibility. He was waiting on God to perform a certain miracle he (Burnett) had devised to prove that he (God) was real. Burnett was expecting this miracle to trigger his decision and get him off the fence.

God *can* perform an individual miracle for a person. But the chances are this miracle would be only a temporary remedy: he would need to do another soon thereafter to prove himself again.

Salvation, remember, is a relationship, a way of living life. It is not a concept to be believed. "Faith" in the New Testament is a verb as well as a noun. It is quite proper to speak of "faithing." "Faithing" involves mental "belief" as we are accustomed to using the term, but it includes much more. Faith means becoming a follower, a disciple. It means living in personal relationship to God himself—not just in theology, but in daily practice. It means learning and living a new way of life with the Author to help you.

When we look at "salvation" in the Bible, we notice immediately that it has three dimensions or tenses to it—past, present, and future. The apostle Paul writes of his own experience at times as if it were entirely past—he has been plucked from destruction as an astronaut from an angry sea. In one of the most eloquent passages of the Bible, Paul says, "By grace you [Christians] *have been saved* through faith" (Eph. 2:8, RSV) and, elsewhere, "Through him [Jesus] we have obtained access to this grace *in which we stand*" (Rom. 5:2, RSV). Most Christians would concur that something irreversible happened to them at some past period in their lives when they came to know Jesus in a changing way.

"Salvation" is also past tense in a historical sense. At a specific point in time, God sent a person named Jesus. He was born under unusual circumstances, lived a life of complete obedience to and fellowship with his heavenly Father, died by Roman crucifixion, and, a short time later, was raised from his grave. Through this happening, the Bible makes plain, God entered history in a unique way and saved it, including us who were to come. God took the initiative. He stepped into our existence to make things right. He spoke to us through his Son.

As disdainful as some sophisticates may be toward it, Christian salvation also has a *future* dimension. Paul speaks of the Holy Spirit as being a guarantee until the Day of Redemption (Eph. 1:14; 4:30). His lengthy discussion of Jesus' second coming (1 Thess. 4-5) connects the hope of future salvation with the end of the age. "For salvation is nearer to us now than when we first believed" (Rom. 13:11, RSV). The apostle John wrote, "We shall be like him, for we shall see him as he is" (1 John 3:2, RSV). The final glory of man, and of the whole creation, must await the final redemption, "the glorious liberty of the children of God," wrote Paul (Rom. 8:18-25, RSV).

This latter passage is unusually significant because it points to the importance and essential unity of the whole created order. It shows God's intention to redeem all his creation—a larger view of salvation than self-centered man sometimes envisions. The early Christians, in short, looked toward a fantastic future after death . . . with Jesus and their fellow believers in a universe operating as God intended. This is salvation in its ultimate dimension.

Oddly enough, many discussions of salvation touch very lightly on the *present* tense. Yet this is really where the action is. The present moment is the only moment any person has. In one sense this is our only opportunity to be saved. Salvation as past action is important. We need to know with finality that we are forgiven and adopted into God's family. We must have this assurance and joy to be able to function lovingly in the present.

The future dimension of our salvation is also tremendously

important. Without the promise of future improvement, the present struggle would at times be hopeless and unbearable. We don't need to feel embarrassed about looking forward to a future reward. Especially if our goal is to be fully functioning persons like Jesus.

We do need, however, as Christians to regularly reestablish the goal for our lives. It is easy to lose our way among the false gods our world offers. The present, then, looms up as being all important in our salvation. This is where the past is expressed. This is where the future is determined. Now is the only moment we have in which to be saved (2 Cor. 6:2). We don't have to wait for the future; we can begin now to become the saved person God has created us to be. We can begin working out our own salvation as we respond to God's working in our lives (Phil. 2:12-13). The forgiveness of the past, the sure promise of the future, and the daily witness of the Spirit free us to love (live "saved") in the present. We cannot postpone the adventure, and perhaps pain, of responding to God's leading *now*—to allow ourselves to see life differently, to place our priorities on spiritual, person values, to be a server as well as a served, to value highly ourselves and all others.

Each of us has the opportunity of participating in a salvation which is uniquely our own. It is inseparably connected with the emergence of the person God wants us to be.

We sometimes still are deeply frustrated by our indecisiveness, discouraged by our failures and sin, pained by our limitations, embarrassed by our differentness, and wounded by the enemy. But we keep working out our salvation—keep faithing—because we know it's right. We continue because we see ourselves slowly, bit-by-bit, becoming more "saved." more a person as Jesus was a person. We experience that our salvation is nearer than when we first believed.

12 How Can I Witness to Students from Different Backgrounds?

Steve

One of the first things college teaches you is that people are different. Kids aren't all alike in high school, but in college they get "curiouser and curiouser." It is a cliché that colleges are full of wierdos, but the fact is that you are often confronted with people so different from yourself that you don't have any notion of where to begin a witness.

The students most obviously different from yourself are those from other countries, especially non-Western countries. Here a lot of differences are clear-cut, but it is wrong to assume that these differences are all superficial. The differences probably go much deeper than you can comprehend unless you've spent a lot of time in an Asian or African country. "Human nature" is not always the same, except that it is always strange. Differences are more than skin deep; they involve basic conceptions of the universe and of deity.

It's like this: If you started rattling off NFL pass-completion statistics to your mother (given a male-chauvinist definition of "mother"), not only would she probably not understand what you were talking about, but furthermore she wouldn't care about it, since her world-view football is a totally irrelevant consideration, just a bunch of rowdy guys beating their heads together. Do you see what I mean? Someone from another culture not only might not *know* about important Christian doctrines, but he might not even see them as important questions. So you need to be patient in witnessing to him, demonstrating by careful thought and a caring life that the question of his relationship to Christ is important.

On the other hand, you don't want to be condescending toward international students. It's a drag for someone to explain things to you that you already know, and it makes you feel, "Boy, he must really think I'm dumb." To return to the NFL analogy: If you've been watching football for years, and your father keeps explaining (every week) what a touchback is, it's a drag. Right? To continue literally: If you're watching football with an international student, don't assume that he knows nothing. He may have been watching for a long time; he may have had lots of explanations before; he may even have boned up on football just to impress American students. If you start trying to explain to him that the Cowboys are a team and even try to explain what cowboys are, that's a drag. And it's an insult. It doesn't take much effort to ask him, "Do you watch much football?" Try to find out how much he *does* know and go from there. Even if he doesn't know much, don't lecture at him. Saying, "Wow, Lilly grabbed the quarterback's face mask! That's a fifteen yard penalty!" comes across a lot better than saying, "That is called a 'face-mask violation.' It's against the rules to grab the face mask. He will be penalized fifteen yards. Do you understand?"

So much for football. But the same thing is true in talking about Christianity. You need to find out how much an international student already knows. He didn't come to the United States because he was uninterested in our culture, and he's not a native in remote jungles. To start out with, "Have you heard of a man we call Jesus Christ?" is pretty insulting. Try to find out how he himself feels about Christianity and talk to him in personal terms as you would talk with another American student. It may take a little more patience, a little more time.

Of course, international students are not the only students with backgrounds very different from your own. You may have opportunities to witness to students from other parts of the country, from other racial groups, from a dope subculture, from a stock-car subculture, from a computer subculture, or from any number of subcultural groups found on campus. In dealing with "different" people, you might remember the two suggestions for relating to students from other cultures: (1) Don't assume that they are just like you. (2) Don't assume that they are ignorant. When you're talking with them about Christianity, try to discover what they know and how they feel.

Perhaps the most important thing in witnessing to a person with a different background is your naturalness, your at-ease-ness. There is a tendency to depersonalize a person who is very different from yourself, and in Christians this tendency is sometimes manifested as trophy-hunting. "Oh, he looks like a Buddhist or something," you say. 'I'm going to convert him." Or you pick out the biggest dope dealer in town to witness to because it will make such a good testimony. Or you look at a math major and imagine yourself saying, "He was nothing but a human computer until I brought him to the Lord." So when you go to talk to them about the humanizing Lord, you relate to them not as humans but as stereotypes: the Oriental, the Pusher, the Brain. Furthermore, you end up acting not as yourself but as the Christian—which is, needless to say, a drag. Unless you are both at ease with who you are and at ease with who the other person is, you will have a hard time sharing Christ's love. Note well: Sharing. Please, if you just want to donate your time and energy to the cause of Christ, go scrub somebody's floor. If you want to witness, love.

Bill

A foreign student, particularly one of a strange (to you) religious heritage, may seem like a very unlikely person to witness to. His ability to communicate in English may be halting, and you may find yourself one of those provincial Americans who must speak English or not at all. Your common ground seems like a postage stamp. After the usual exchange about home, family, academic plans, vocational plans, and opinion of the United States, your conversation comes to a grinding halt. You panic inside. You can't seem to come up with anything of interest; he offers nothing, also.

At this point you feel a leading from some place to go elsewhere —anywhere! You wonder how you can converse about God when you can't get anything else going. But it's at this point that your real concern can show itself. If you can hang in as a friend, even as a quiet friend, relax, and be yourself, you'll find a bond developing between you, and the conversation will gradually take care of itself. Visualize yourself in your foreign friend's shoes. What if you were in another country where practically no one spoke English? The person who was your friend through ease and unease would help immensely.

Some international students may be critical and/or cynical, but these are definitely a small minority. Most are humbly wanting to know all they can and are painfully aware of their inadequacies. They are looking for a place they can feel at home and a person they know to be a friend.

Talking about religion—even a forthright sharing of the gospel— is not as difficult with foreign students as it might appear. Most visitors to this country want to learn about our religion, along with other aspects of our culture. In fact, some will be disappointed if they don't find out about Christianity while they are here. As your friendship begins to develop, you will find religion a natural topic to discuss. Your new friend will probably appreciate your invitation to attend your church and to be in the homes of church members. He will usually count it an honor to meet the pastor and other church leaders. He will enjoy getting to know your friends in church and in the campus Christian fellowship.

Don't expect every international student to be knowledgable about what is supposed to be the predominant religion of his country. You know how inaccurate it would be to assume every American abroad is thoroughly conversant with Christianity. Further, the world religion picture is in a chaotic condition. Some oriental expected-to-be-Buddhist countries have many Christians, both Roman Catholic and Protestant. Some eastern religions have undergone changes and subdivisions in recent years so the adherents no longer fit the textbook description. Science, education, war, and technology have upset the culture in many places, making the former religions seem out of place.

Vietnam, Thailand, Korea, Japan, and Taiwan are all countries where the ancestral religious roots have been dislodged, particularly among the young people.

The result is that large numbers of students who come here to study are uncommitted or have loose religious ties. Perhaps their parents have a religion; they do not claim one.

So, far from having a difficult situation, you may find yourself with a new friend who is open—even seeking—and eager to listen to a new friend he is beginning to love and trust.

As your friendship grows, you should find yourself becoming more and more interested in your international friend's outlook, background, religion, and culture. You may want to learn his language, eat his foods, and/or appreciate his art and music. You probably will want to converse and read about the traditional religions of his country and parents. As you get to know these things, you will see better how communication about Christ is sounding to him. You will know when he is interested in Christ for his own life.

This interest may come sooner than you think. One of the most meaningful experiences you can have in college is to attend a church-sponsored international student retreat. A closeness in a Christian context usually develops that is hard to have on campus. At the closing session of one such two-day retreat recently, a Taiwanese student openly and directly asked a Christian Taiwanese, "How did you become a Christian? How can I?"

Try to include non-Christian students in your church and campus group fellowship and activities. The spirit and activities of the group often help immensely to clarify the meaning of Christianity.

As to American students with nontraditional religious orientation, their number is diverse and growing. I know of no way to begin to learn to respond to everyone of these "types" of people. A good guideline is to find out where the person is in his thinking and to discuss your differences and/or give your witness on biblical grounds.

Use the Bible as you think and talk together. Let it be the focus of your search.

In the process of sticking to the Bible, however, you probably will run into students who don't put much stock in the Scripture, though the percentage of students rejecting the Bible is probably at an all-time low. You may want to think through witnessing to this particular kind of person.

A campus minister in Texas some years ago was fond of saying, "So what if the student says he doesn't believe the Bible is the sword of the Lord. Stick him with it, anyway! He'll find it cuts!" The minister's statement always struck me as being a little insensitive, but he had a "point." There is an authenticity, a plainness of thought, a singleness of Spirit about the Scriptures which really communicate spiritual truth. You don't need to beat a person into submission with a barrage of Scripture verses, but you can honestly say that you can explain better out of the Bible than with just your own words. Then read and explain as you go portions of the Bible which seem pertinent to your conversation.

To focus on the Bible doesn't mean you have to use only the Scriptures. The Spirit can use your own reasoning and phrasing. In some cases your rephrase or paraphrase or general summary of a biblical teaching will be more helpful than reading a lengthy passage.

And when you read, read from a modern translation. Find one you like and use it.

In most instances, when a person says he doesn't accept the Bible, he probably means that he believes it has nothing to say to *him*. Occasionally, however, you may talk with a person who really has serious doubts about the origin and validity of the Bible—so much so that the doubts raise a formidable barrier to his Christian belief. This is not usually the case, but it may happen. To help this person, and to feel more secure in your own position, you may want to read a book on Christian apologetics which emphasizes the historical, archaeological, and other support for the validity of the biblical evidence. An impressive amount of support exists. You are not out on a limb on faith alone—far from it! Two of many books you can read are *Evidence that Demands a Verdict* by Josh McDowell and *The New Testament Documents: Are They Reliable?* by F. F. Bruce.

You may feel as if you are called upon to defend God himself in some of your encounters with students who think vastly different from you. But as you are able to see these students as real persons with reasons for being as they are, you will find yourself entering one interesting adventure after another . . . with God. He is actively working in and through your relationships to change both you and your friends into his likeness. Don't shrink from the opportunity to be a part of God's working.

Steve: It seems to me we have a tendency to witness to people who are like ourselves and people who are attractive. Is this good?

Bill: I'd say it is both good and bad. No one can be equally effective in understanding and communicating with all people. I think most of us can be relevant easier with persons in our general niche in life. I don't believe anyone can witness more effectively to a college student than another student.

Still, if we shut ourselves off to those who don't look or act like us, we are limiting God and running the danger of being respecters of persons.

Steve: The tendency worries me a little. The natural rapport we feel with some people can be a God-given oneness which helps communication. But it seems to me it can also be selfish—either self-adoration by admiring someone like ourselves or wanting to be associated with someone who is attractive.

I wonder sometimes, on the other hand, if we are not afraid of being associated with the "wrong" subcultural group; that is, freaks, intellectuals, hicks, nondaters, and so forth.

Bill: Jesus was amazing, wasn't he, in his ability and effort to communicate with everyone—religious leaders, political leaders, wealthy tax collectors, fishermen, revolutionaries, lepers, prostitutes, the poor, the blind, children, homekeepers? His disciples represented quite a range of background and temperament. If he showed favoritism, it seems to have been to the humble, the downrodden, the poor in spirit. This has to be a warning to us not to get lost in the academic world.

Steve: Even on campus I think we ought to learn to witness to those who are different from us. We ought to force ourselves out of our normal associations and try to broaden our understanding and witness. There is a danger that a Baptist Student Union or other Christian group can be so homogeneous socially that it limits its witness. A person might feel that in order to become a Christian he has to cut his hair just so, wear certain clothes, be white middle-class, and drink a particular soft drink.

13 How Important Is Study?

Steve

It's the inevitable question. You're sitting at your desk with the books piled up and it's late, late—everything is late: papers to write, books to read, and you—late arriving at the person you must be. The feeling creeps up, seeping from the books themselves; it is a sense of time gone by and nothing done, a world gone by and nothing changed, a world awaiting your witness and here you sit. "I could be at a prayer meeting," you think. I could be out visiting, serving God—and here I sit. The campus, the world is lovely, dark, and deep. But you have promises to keep, and books to read before you sleep.

Studies often seem irrelevant to your goals in life, and you ask yourself, "What good is this doing me?" The question should become, "Is this God's will?" That is a good question. If God doesn't want you to be in college, then you'd better get out. But you have to be sure you're asking the right question. You don't quit school because you're not having fun all the time or because you're impatient to win souls or because it would make you feel more spiritual. I was close to leaving school in my freshman year, all set to become a full-time Jesus freak. But I discovered that what I was seeking was not God's will but spiritual security and the emotional gratifications of evangelistic activity. God had a harder thing for me. He wanted me to stay at school.

I make a statement: *Study is work*. It is not something you do instead of work. It is the work to which God has called you. Brothers and sisters, do I make myself clear? In trendier collegiate Christian circles, it sometimes becomes trendy to say, "I have to study so much I don't have time to work for the Lord." Oh, my. Need I repeat? Study *is* work for the Lord. There is no need for a tension between study and work, since they are identical; there is a tension between study and *play*. I think "play" can encompass a lot of Christian fellowship, a lot of self-serving witnessing, a lot of Christian music—a lot of stuff we like to call spiritual "work." Of course, all work and no play makes Jack a dull boy; but we fool ourselves if we label as "work" the things we do just for fun. All play and no work will also make Jack a dull boy.

You need to be certain that college study is God's will for you. Obviously, many people go to college who don't belong there. But if you conclude that God does want you in college, then you ought to take it as seriously as you would any other work for God. A lot of people who would work hard on a factory job earning money will just mess around in college. This shows, I suppose, that they are willing to work for money but not for God. When there are no rewards other than God's approval, they goof off.

God uses study to shape you, to help you become someone. You may or may not be learning specific skills which you will use later, but you are certainly learning discipline and learning about your own limitations, about man's limitations and man's knowledge, about how God has worked in history and in creation. You are at least learning that answers do not come easily. That may be the most important lesson of all.

Bill

A person's peers exhibit a curious kind of attitude toward him most of his days. They try to keep him from excelling . . . particularly in studies. The alert student is subject to name-calling from his earliest years. "Teacher's pet," "book worm," "four eyes," and "intellect" are a few of the names that were hurled in derision at the more astute persons in my public school classes. It was unusual in my high school for a person to do well in both grades and popularity. We tended to resent and/or fear the high achiever and tried to whittle or to shame him down to our size.

Perhaps this tendency is merely human nature. A person wants to cut down another whom he feels inferior to. Society punishes people for their nonconformity. The person who relentlessly pursues perfection will suffer not only from his own discipline but also from the criticisms of others. We are uncomfortable with a person who isn't like us, who does not play our games of mediocrity, friendliness, and mock humility.

That is, until a person "makes it." After he "arrives" and is established as an "expert" or "genius" or "star," he suddenly becomes a hero. All the doors are open to him. He can do no wrong . . . even in fields outside his expertise.

The pressure to conform eliminates a lot of potential high achievers. They value the esteem of their contemporaries so highly they fail to live up to their full potential. Do you ever wonder how miserable a life a successful male concert pianist must have lived as a boy? Even dedicated athletes are chided in a reverse way as being "animals," "jocks," and "dumbbells."

Anti-excellence is especially widespread toward intellectual pursuits. It's called anti-intellectualism, and the woods are full of it. I'm sure the expression, "A little learning is a dangerous thing" must have originated in relation to a college student. Maybe because we still fancy ourselves rugged pioneers, the typical United States workingman tends to blame everything bad on the educated persons among us.

Perhaps this is particularly true in religion. Religion sometimes is the last reservoir of a society's folkways and the most resistant to change of any area of culture. Several years ago when a friend of mine left home to go to college, his small church came by, one by one, at the close of worship one Sunday to tell him good-bye. The chief deacon was the last to come. As he took Kenneth's hand, he looked him hard in the eyes and said; "Don't go. You'll lose your faith."

This anti-intellectual attitude still influences you and your friends and relatives. You may want to make good grades or get a good job. This is not too uncommon. But you are a rare individual if you are determined to be the *best in your field*, no matter what it costs you. Yet the apostle Paul admonished, "Whatever your task, work heartily, as serving the Lord and not men" (Col. 3:23, RSV). Paul certainly practiced what he preached at this point. He gave himself unbelievably to live out his calling as apostle.

How could developing one's mental capacities fail to be thoroughly Christian? Ideas have consequences. Today's ideas form tomorrow's world. How better can a Christian transform the world for the good than by having superior thoughts?

But thinking *is* work. The more creative it is, the more discipline it requires, as a general rule. The White Queen's statement to Alice that "Why, sometimes I've believed as many as six impossible things before breakfast" is so funny because it is so ridiculous. Creative thinking requires knowledge . . . of both content and process. Inventions, great novels, peace settlements, brilliant speeches—any sort of excellence—don't just *happen* before breakfast. Someone pays the price for them. Doesn't it sound logical that God expects his professing followers to be doing some of this?

The church of Jesus should receive anyone into its fellowship. It should welcome a person and warm him and love him and accept him . . . whatever his strengths and weaknesses may be. But the church should allow no one of its fellowship to rest easy with mediocrity and easy achievement and lack of discipline. Members should shame, cajole, challenge, reward, and support one another to live out their gifts as completely as possible.

Steve: Bill, I think we've made our point that study is important. But everyone can't make straight A's, right? I'd say studies become too important when they make you constantly nervous or drive you into isolation.

Bill: Right! Each person must live up to his own calling. I think we have to take the long look at what God wants us to do. He's not calling every Christian to think world-transforming thoughts. But he is calling some. Every Christian must listen to God and build his own life with God's guidance. We need to remember that many people around us, even our friends, will want us to give ourselves to all sorts of activities. And we need some variety—some fellowship, some play. But no one can do everything. He must choose. A person can't let his life get away from him. He must keep it focused on his peculiar, God-given gifts.

Steve: So the real goal is developing your gifts to serve God. I guess that involves a lot of love and trust, as well as work. And those who have academic gifts shouldn't feel better than those with gifts in other areas. It gets back to a manner of accepting diversity in the body of Christ.

Bill: You seem to feel pretty strongly, Steve, about a person's not going off the deep end on study.

Steve: Yes. God is also using a person's relationship with people in college. He wants to use everyone to witness and to minister to others, and no one must decide that he is just too busy studying to help anyone else. A person cannot grow without sharing. It's again a question of balance.

But in balancing the various parts of his life, a student must take care in determining what parts are work and what parts are play, and he must take care to counterbalance natural tendencies. If he tends to play around, he must make a disciplined effort to schedule more time for work. If he tends to work very hard and isolate himself, he should schedule more time for developing relationships and having fun. And no one should be so worried about balance that he cannot act. Schedules should be flexible enough to allow the Holy Spirit to lead to unexpected opportunities. Those serendipities in study and relationships are the best part of any schedule.

14 How Can I Deal with Cheating and Dishonesty?

Steve

You want to say it doesn't exist, but you can't. It keeps cropping up in unexpected places, in the nicest people. Sometimes it's obvious, like when the guy next to you in an exam is craning his neck to look over that smart girl's shoulder, or when he pulls a slip of paper from his pocket. But usually academic dishonesty is more subtle, more borderline, more gray than black.

"Hey, old buddy," your roommate begs, "you know I didn't finish that lab on romantic interest in marijuana-smoking pigeons last week. Could I just check your data to fill in some of this stuff? It's due in an hour."

Or: "I've heard that old Professor Huffenstrut gives the same final exam every year. Didn't you take his course on 'Square Dance and Cosmology in the Pre-Columbian Era' last year? How about letting me look at the finals?"

Or: "Man, I'm never going to finish this French homework. How do you say, 'Jacques, who is visiting in Paris, looks for a restroom in the Eiffel Tower'?"

Or: "Didn't you do a paper last term on 'The Victory of William the Junker at the Battle of Haste'? It's a strange coincidence, but I'm doing a paper on the same thing for a different professor. You wouldn't mind letting me see your masterpiece, would you?"

There are more ways to be dishonest with professors than your fine Christian mind would want to imagine. Most of them fall under the heading of *plagiarism*, which is representing someone else's work as your own. There's nothing wrong with letting your roommate read your paper, but if he says he wrote it, *that* is wrong. Unless, of course, he puts a footnote at the end of the whole paper: Adapted from a paper by my colleague, E. Z. Mark.

Students who plagiarize don't advertise it. They might not even realize that they are doing anything wrong. When they come to you, they don't say, "Help me cheat." They say, "Help me." Your first reaction may be that helping is the Christian thing to do. But you have to consider both the school rules and what is ultimately best for the one in need.

Many schools have an honor code which you have to take into consideration. Often it is in the form of specific guidelines which each student accepts as a contract. You are obligated as a Christian to follow the honor code as you are obligated to fulfill a contract or keep a promise.

Of course, there may be times when it would help *you* to help yourself to another person's work. But there are three things you ought to keep in mind: First, the restrictions of the honor code itself must be obeyed. Second, you should be able to be completely honest with your teachers about your work. Third, you should consider whether or not this plagiarism will help you to learn. Anything that will decrease the amount you learn is unethical, since it is not making full use of the gifts God has given you.

Bill

Cheating and dishonesty have been around the academic scene for a long time. Occasionally a famous athlete will get canned for cheating, or a national magazine will run an expose' of outrageous cribbing practices on campus. But, by and large, cheating and dishonesty do not seem either as horrendous or as exciting as other forms of campus sins. Very often Christians approach them with a sort of ho-hum attitude: "Why bring that up? Let's get to something *important.*"

This indifference toward personal honesty is a bad mistake. Personal honesty comes close to being synonymous with personal integrity. If a person isn't honest, he is askew at the center of his being.

Honesty is a basic concern of the biblical writers. Three of the Ten Commandments (as far back as that!) touch on dishonesty or the motives for it. Jesus' strongest denunciations of sin were to hypocrites, who played games, who pretended to be something they weren't. On the other hand, Jesus commended several persons—who were not considered "religious"—because of their simple honesty.

Paul continually held up honesty as a transparent trait for early Christians. "Putting away falsehood," he wrote, "let every one speak truth with his neighbor, for we are members one of another" (Eph. 4:25, RSV). "Do not lie to one another," Paul wrote to the Colossians (3:9, RSV).

The clear intent of all the New Testament writers is that Christian believers should live lives of complete purity and sincerity.

There are at least *four* reasons we need to be concerned about personal integrity.

One reason is in the word *integrity* itself. The root meaning is "wholeness" or "oneness." A person who is dishonest, who deceives others, can never be quite at peace within himself. As long as he uses subterfuges, he cannot come to terms with himself as he really is, with his weaknesses and strengths. He is relying on outside props. Paul wrote, "For if any one thinks he is something when he is nothing, he deceives himself. But let each one test his own work, and then his reason to boast will be in himself alone and not in his neighbor. For each man will have to bear his own load" (Gal. 6:3-5, RSV).

Somewhere along the line you have doubtless been taught that pride and boasting are wrong. Certainly they *are* if they are either obnoxious or false. But some pride and boasting are healthy. Even if you never share it with anyone (which may be the path of wisdom), you need to experience doing something well and knowing that you did it. Cheating and dishonesty pull the rug out from under your sense of accomplishment. You can't really be sure you can do it alone. A side effect is that cheating becomes habit forming—your lack of self-confidence inclines you toward cheating the next time.

A second reason personal honesty is important is reflected in the second half of Paul's statement in Ephesians 4:25: "for we are members one of another" (RSV). To be dishonest is to destroy community. How can a person deceive a member of his own body? Paul's injunction was directed toward a church, the body of Christ. But Christians should be about building community wherever they are, not erecting barriers that make rapport more difficult.

Third, there's no escaping the matter of witness for Christ—the positive witness of a life of scrupulous honesty and the negative witness of a cheater. Honesty seems universally to be recognized as a vital cornerstone of human society. Even agnostics believe Christians ought to be honest. I have trouble with the credibility of a human rights worker I know. I believe in *what he's doing*, but I don't know about *him*. When he was a divinity school student and I was an unholy engineering undergraduate, he and I washed dishes together in the school cafeteria. He was a goof off, and besides that, he stole their soap.

Fourth, the kind of undue concern for grades which cheating sometimes signifies is a form of idolatry—the worship of the grade points or the diploma. Taking matters into your own hands dishonestly betrays a lack of faith in God's care for you . . . or an earlier presumption that God would do-it-all for you.

One difficult thing about cheating and some other forms of campus dishonesty: The issue isn't always clear cut. Even Christians don't agree on what's dishonest. The events surrounding the Watergate break-ins illustrated, among other things, how common it is to rationalize wrong into right, to go from unsullied to unsure to unsavory.

"A one-time theft is not really stealing."

"A lot of school work is Mickey Mouse anyway; I'm going to be ethical when I get out of school."

"Surely it's better for me to get a little help on this final exam

81

rather than not graduate and disappoint everybody, including my future employer."

"The prof is impossible, unreasonable. If he were halfway decent, I wouldn't have to put notes in my sneakers."

"Everybody else in the class cheats. I don't stand a chance if I don't."

All these statements or their facsimiles have seemed reasonable to various students at various times.

Steve

The fact that cheating seems reasonable to some students causes a lot of problems in relating to them. Even if you yourself don't go out and cheat, you're probably going to get stuck by people who do. There are two main problems that arise: turning them down and turning them in.

I don't think there is any question that helping someone to cheat is immoral. Just as the cheater is acting out of selfish motives, you help the cheater because you selfishly want his continued friendship. Besides, conspiring together to defraud the society at large will tend both to separate the two of you from that society and to separate you from one another by lessening your trust. If someone asks you to help him cheat, you simply have to turn him down. But how?

It's not easy, since your natural reaction would be to go along. You may have trouble getting up the nerve to say no, but be careful that you don't overcompensate. Once you decide to turn him down, you may swing all the way in a negative direction and turn him inside out. It won't do much good to stand up and scream, "Liar, liar, pants on fire, hang yourself on a telephone wire!" The motivation for our righteousness is love, and if we forget that love we lose our righteousness.

You need to remember that cheating seems reasonable to the person who wants to try it. Talk the problem out with him and try to understand his rationalizations. If you can, point out his fallacies and explain to him why you think helping him would be wrong. I *know* this is hard, but it is crucial that you maintain your integrity as a Christian in such a situation.

In some schools, there is a further complication. Honor codes usually require that students report any violation they witness. This might mean turning in a friend of yours. At Princeton, I've honestly never seen anyone cheat on a test; so I've never had to face this dilemma. But it seems to me that if you have pledged yourself to obey the honor code, you really have no choice but to fulfill that promise. You might try not to look around in exams and make an effort *not* to notice what other students are doing. If you *do* see someone cheating, however, you're just stuck, ethically. You'd be bound to turn the guilty student in. After all, all you can do is pray for peace about it and try to help the student in any way you can. It might help you, just from an instinct for self-preservation, to remember that if anyone else saw that you witnessed the violation and you don't report it, you can be in big trouble, too. If you can't bring yourself to obey the law for any other reason, obey it out of fear.

14½ (What Is "Christian" Morality, Anyway?)

Bill

Since we're dealing with "moral issues" in this portion of the book, perhaps it would be good to take a look at the whole business of making moral decisions. Is a Christian obligated to keep the "rules" regardless of the circumstances and to always avoid every appearance of evil? Or, should he weigh every situation individually before he decides? Is there, after all, a Christian approach to making moral decisions?

Though it is not extremely popular among college students, one approach to moral decision-making holds that a Christian can and should develop a set of rules by which he lives. These rules are based upon the Bible and are devised to protect the Christian from sin. This approach to morality is called *legalism*. While the term itself has become distasteful to most modern persons, we should not dismiss the approach just because it *sounds* bad.

Legalism actually has several advantages for the decision-maker. For one thing it simplifies deciding. If a certain activity is determined to be wrong, it continues to be wrong under all circumstances. If lying is wrong, there is not ever any set of conditions that can justify lying. No time or effort need ever be wasted on this type decision.

Second, legalism leads to consistency and discipline in living.

The legalist may not treat persons according to their circumstances, but he will probably treat all persons the same. He will tend to be consistent in his own behavior because he will not rationalize or waiver between opinions. The legalist will probably be extremely well disciplined because he is uncomfortable with loose ends and flabbiness in any form.

But legalism as an approach to morality has some weaknesses. In *Morality and the Mass Media*, Kyle Haselden lists several:

First, legalism places priority on externals. A person is good or bad according to whether or not he keeps the rules. His reasons and motives are of no consequence. The reason he doesn't murder may be because he is afraid he himself will be killed. No matter. He is righteous because he didn't actually kill someone.

Second, legalism is dangerous because it tends to major on the negative rather than the positive. Human freedom is played down; conformity and restriction are exalted. God becomes a kind of cosmic scorekeeper.

Third, legalism tends to eliminate the personal. It majors on keeping the rules rather than relating to the Ruler. The code-keeper's insistence upon the law may actually alienate him from God. Further, legalism imposes the same conduct, the same response to life from all persons. It eliminates the distinctive qualities of individual personality.

Fourth, legalism tends to major on trivialities. The degree of good in life increasingly becomes a matter of complying with more and more minute regulations.

Fifth, legalism takes the wonder out of life. As Haselden says, the legalist "enters the unknown future, holding, not the hand of God, but a manual of conduct." In fact, legalism majors on *past* rules and conduct and is to some degree closed to the *present* and *future*. Ultimately this means that the rule follower is not open to the Holy Spirit's leading. As Paul said, the letter kills the Spirit.

At the other extreme from legalism is an approach to moral decision-making called *relativism*. "Situation ethics" became popular a few years ago as a theory of "Christian" relativism. Relativism in general is the concept that there are no rules in moral decision-making: everything depends on the particular situation.

One popular Christianized version of this concept holds that love is the only possible guide to true morality. Every situation must be evaluated in terms of its effect upon the people involved; then the loving (moral) decision to make is the one which benefits most of the people involved. No consideration should be given to rules or principles, according to situation ethics, because these tend to ignore the needs of individual people.

It is possible according to this ethical approach that under certain circumstances love will demand that a Christian lie, steal, or commit adultery. And if it is the loving thing to do, then it is not bad, whatever the act; it is good, because the motive, the attitude is what's important. Killing a person, if done as the most loving act in a particular situation, should not be considered a "necessary evil" or the "lesser of two evils," but it should be judged as positive good.

Proponents of this view cite Jesus as the prime teacher of this approach. He broke the ritualistic rules of his day to help people. He went wherever he was needed regardless of the taboos he crossed. He continually held up love as both the essence of God and the chief ingredient of the abundant life.

The situation ethics form of relativism became popular during the growth of permissiveness in our society. No doubt it represents a reaction to legalism. It came as a welcome relief to many who were chafing under restrictions to their behavior which they felt to be both limiting and religion-based. Situation ethics has continued to be the basis on which many people say they operate: no rules, no prescribed behavior; live life spontaneously, doing the loving thing as it appears; think strictly in terms of the present, not worrying much about the past or future implications of the decision.

Compared to legalism, this form of situation ethics obviously looks good to a generation seeking freedom of personal expression. It has some conspicuous strengths. Its statements major on love and freedom. It focuses on persons rather than rules. It calls forth man's need to make moral decisions rather than just uncritically to follow the dictates of the past. It seems to treat decision-makers as mature, responsible adults. It serves a useful purpose in counteracting legalism.

But somehow situation ethics turned out to be an overstatement. Perhaps what its advocates intended to be a needed emphasis was applied too universally and too radically. Perhaps they didn't express themselves clearly enough. Undoubtedly, they overestimated man's maturity and underestimated his self-centeredness. And they, like the legalists, did not leave much room for the leadership of the Holy Spirit.

For whatever reason, situation ethics seemed to promote irresponsibility as well as responsibility. Possibly because of a superficial understanding, the idea of love in situation ethics became a justification of Ernest Hemingway's philosophy: If it *feels* good, it *is* good. It seems to support the thought that many young people were already beginning to have: "If I don't see any harm in it, why not do it? My situation is not like any other. Who can tell me what is right or wrong?"

So, doubtless, situation ethics became the philosophical base for using drugs, for having premarital sex, for misleading parents and other authorities. It said to people, whether it intended to or not: "Most of the things people have been calling bad can be good. Nothing is always bad except not loving."

"Great," mused the campus swinger. "Who could be more loving than I?"

"You may be right," replied the reluctant coed. "I am feeling warm inside myself."

Most Christians believe that a moral decision should be made in light of the situation that surrounds it. To that extent they are situationists. But to understand the true "situation" is to look beyond just the factors and persons of the immediate moment. It is to be aware of guiding principles. It is to estimate the effect of the decision on persons not present. It is to take a long-range look at its effect on oneself. It is to recognize oneself and one's situation as a part of the total moral situation of the church and of the larger society. It is recognizing that what appears at the moment to be love might really be wishful thinking, vanity, selfishness, lust, impulse, and/or short-sightedness.

Christian morality must be lived out somewhere in between the two extremes of legalism and relativism. Its *objective* is to help persons be and do all that God intends for them. Its *method* is love, defined as doing that which helps us and our fellows to be our best. Its *arena* is freedom—freedom to act for the good of persons, ourselves, and others. Its *source* is God, who has shown us a true moral man in Jesus and who empowers us by his Spirit to act as he did.

Authentic morality is not enslaved to the past, but it recognizes the folly of ignoring it. The Christian tries to respond in love to the need of the moment, but he acknowledges a person's need for structure and guiding principles and consistency of character. Rather than looking at every situation as completely new and unexplored, the Christian seeks to employ what he's learned from experience and from others. He reasons as best he can what action is most loving for the most people, but he knows he has limits; he looks beyond his reason to One who has greater love, broader understanding, and sounder judgment.

As Haselden points out, authentic morality takes its cue from Matthew 22:37-40. Asked about the greatest commandment, the heart of religion, Jesus replied: "You shall love the Lord your God with all your heart, and with all your soul, and with all your mind. This is the great and first commandment. And the second is like it, You shall love your neighbor as yourself" (RSV).

In this passage Jesus clearly establishes love for God and the desire to do his will as the first principle of a Christian's life. He calls for love, not law or duty, to be the basis for behavior. And, though the questioner didn't ask for it, Jesus gave him the second commandment ... perhaps because he didn't want it separated from the first: "You shall love your neighbor as yourself."

This sequence seems to tell us that people are more important than anything else in the created order, and that love for God and love for people go together. Christian morality is concerned about good coming to people—individual persons with whom we have contact and people we will never know.

Christian morality must ask beneath-the-surface questions about how actions of school, business, government, and church effect people. The criterion for success of any endeavor or any institution is not how big or wealthy it is, but how specifically and widely it helps people.

Steve: We still have a real problem here in determining what it means to "help" people—help them be what? Or, help them do what? It is clear that we ought to act in an unselfish manner, but before we can decide how to act, we have to decide how we ought to help people. Are we trying to help them know God? be healthy? be happy? be undisturbed and placid? serve God? serve their society? what? Judas says that the way to help is to sell the ointment and give it to the poor. Jesus says that the way to help is to allow a woman to worship, squandering her money. Especially in the affluent parts of our society, helping someone physically may not be helping him spiritually. Maybe someone *needs* to suffer a little.

I'm not proposing any definite answers, but I think we need to get away from the stereotyped notions of what "helping" is.

Bill: In general, and that may not be what you want, I think God's goal for every person is that he become all that he is capable of becoming—that he be the most creative, loving, and effective person possible. This implies that he be in tune with God and be together as a person as much as possible for him.

Our jobs as Christians are to help persons be the most complete persons—the most truly human persons—they can be. As you say, this may mean withholding something instead of giving something. It may mean confronting someone instead of placidly letting something pass. It probably means being honest with everyone. This requires a depth of love, a depth of involvement that is difficult to practice.

I referred to Jesus as God's example of moral man, because I believe he's the best clue we have to what Christian morality is. It's a life lived in obedience to God and service to persons. This is really what the whole New Testament is about, but especially Jesus' life.

Steve: Another thing that bothered me in your description of morality is this: Isn't love more than a method? I think my view would be more mystically oriented than that. It seems to me that love is a manifestation of God himself and that those who love are to that extent participating in his existence. I refer you to 1 John 4:7-8: "Love is of God, and he who loves is born of God and knows God. He who does not love does not know God; for God is love" (RSV).

Bill: I'm not sure I understand what you mean. I don't want to get lost in wordiness, but I may be seeing it differently. In the first place, I didn't mean to be saying that love is *only* method; it is more, but I do believe love is a method, a way, an approach to relating to people.

Love in the abstract has no meaning. John also said, "By this we know love, that he laid down his life for us; and we ought to lay down our lives for the brethren. But if any one has this world's goods and sees his brother in need, yet closes his heart against him, how does God's love abide in him? Little children, let us not love in word or speech but in deed and truth" (1 John 3:16-18, RSV).

One other comment. I think of God as being a person who loves rather than being personal love itself. We may disagree here. I believe the idea of God encompasses love, but I don't believe it's correct to say "love is God."

Steve: Of course I believe God is a person who is more than love. But I'd say that while our conception of love in the abstract may have no meaning for us, God's love has existed eternally, with or without an object. A part of this eternal love is manifested in human acts of love, but its fullest manifestation was in Christ, so it is through him that we understand what love is. Divine love in the abstract is hardly meaningless; it is only because our human acts of love involve that divine abstract that they have any meaning at all. Oh, Bill, I'm getting too philosophical for my own baggy britches.

Bill: It seems to me you have a good point, but your britches *are* a little baggy.

15 How Can I Deal with Alcohol and Drugs?

Steve

It's not as easy as you might think. You can't just stand on your family and church tradition and say, "That's wrong because I was raised to believe it's wrong." Today's society forces a student to think about alcohol and drugs and make a personal decision. You can't depend on propaganda and scare tactics to make your decision for you; you just can't believe that one sip or one toke will ruin your life. There are too many nice people doing too many illicit things, and there are too many apparently wholesome opportunities for participation for you to brush them off without thought.

I'm not telling you to go out and try everything, but I *am* telling you to think about *why you don't* do certain things. Young people in conservative churches are not often encouraged to think through ethical questions in which there is no clear biblical imperative. We are expected to accept a dogmatic position which may prove to be an embarrassment to us if we haven't reasoned out a moral position.

The problem that seems most difficult here is the moderate use of alcohol. There has been a tendency in conservative denominations to equate Christianity with teetotalism. This kind of equation can hurt your witness, because you can get bogged down in a discussion of alcohol when you ought to discuss Jesus, and because someone might reject Christianity as nothing more than simplistic moralism. Actually, total abstinence is more a part of our own specific culture than a part of Christianity. Some Christian students are surprised to learn that not *all* Christians are abstainers and that some Christians they admire very much are drinkers (and even use wine in church, for heaven's sake). They are also surprised to learn that historically the church has not required abstinence. An undue emphasis on teetotalism can lead to unnecessary divisions in a campus fellowship.

So, you may say, am I telling you to go out and get drunk? Of course not. Don't play games with me. We know that the Bible clearly tells us to avoid drunkenness, and it's easy to see the effect of drunkenness on other students. They look foolish, they insult people, they make a mess, they sometimes deteriorate physically, and they certainly don't glorify God. Well, then, am I telling you to go out and drink moderately? No. You are certainly free to choose the way of abstinence. That is no doubt the way of least danger. But I do think that you should allow others freedom of choice in this matter, and that you should not make total abstinence a prerequisite for relationship with God or yourself. Christians are, after all, free from religious law; we have no right to impose nonbiblical standards on others.

Christians are not, however, free from civil law; and we are told to submit ourselves to legal authorities. This principle makes it a lot easier for us to make a decision about using illegal drugs. Personally, antidrug laws are a great relief to me. They give me a clear ethical basis for abstaining from things my tradition teaches me to reject. Of course, there are other reasons for rejecting marijuana, psychedelics, and narcotics: physical damage from some drugs, lack of scientific evidence about effects, and the obvious psychological effects on people you know. There's another reason that's important to me, although I've never heard it mentioned. It seems to me that these drugs are outside the mainstream of Western civilization, and although it may classify me as a secret archconservative, that matters to me. I mean, the great saints of the church and the great Christian writers never smoked marijuana or opium or mushrooms. Christianity never incorporated Oriental drug-cults; mystic states were achieved without the use of hallucinogenics. I want to place myself in the mainstream of the tradition of the saints, and that is a tradition which does not include drugs.

Bill

The problem of whether or not you should drink and how much is both simpler and more complicated than evaluating the biblical material about drinking. But that's not a bad place to start. The biblical record is a pretty mixed bag. It makes an interesting study, but we don't have the space here to do justice to it. Why don't you do Your Very Own Biblical Study on drinking? Look up "wine," "drink," and "drunk" (and their families) in a moderately thorough Bible concordance and get to studying.

Your problem is simpler, because a lot of the biblical material has to do with customs and cultures and conditions we don't have any more. Of the many references, only a few have direct bearing on today's world and your decision. Your Very Own Biblical Study is going to give you some good background. It's going to generally show you that:

1. Wine was a common drink for both ancient and medieval Israelites. The Mediterranean area is ideal for fruit growing. The early Hebrews had vineyards and fields. From early days, wine and grain were staple crops. Fathers (like Isaac) blessed their children by intoning bounty of grain and wine.

2. Wine had ritualistic significance. They made drink offerings using wine.

3. Wine was forbidden the Nazarites, and top priests when on duty in the tabernacle.

4. Wine was used as a medicine.

5. Both Old and New Testament writers warn about the dangers of drinking intoxicants; the New Testament takes a firm stand against drunkenness.

I have oversimplified this, so please do Your Very Own Biblical Study, still. It's fascinating.

Now. Your problem is also more complicated than a simple examination of biblical drinking customs because your world is different. You can't slickly transfer even first-century mores to now, much less early nomadic Hebrew mores, without trying to take the cultural differences into consideration. You do not consider it Christian to have several wives and concubines, for instance, even though polygamy was a common practice among Old Testament patiarchs and kings.

Your decision is complicated by some factors that make drinking seem very appealing.

Moderate drinking is becoming increasingly a part of the typical young-adult life-style. Particularly, wine is becoming a familiar part both of student get-togethers and of simple meals.

As you have observed it, drinking in moderation may not seem to be harmful to your friends. In fact, it may appear to add a note of festivity and enjoyment to many of their activities. They reason that liquor is a part of God's creation, put here for man's pleasure.

To some persons, perhaps brought up in a legalistic environment, drinking represents a step toward freedom and self-determination.

The liquor industry has a way of making drinking look very "in." "All you need to be what you always dreamed of," its advertising seems to say, "is a bottle of 'Lunchers,' a chunk of ceddar cheese, and a long, thin candle." And, in truth, drinking may help persons to be a more integral part of certain groups.

Your decision is further complicated by some factors that are disturbing. The biblical case for abstinence is based heavily on applying the biblical idea of love to modern conditions.

First, we have a serious alcohol problem in this country. It's getting more and more serious. Few, if any, of these problem drinkers started out to be. But their lives are being ruined, nonetheless, and our society isn't doing much to help them. It's hard to believe that that pretty young thing with the bouncy curls and sparkling eyes drinking that bubbly wine will be a desperate slave to it in ten years. But it happens all the time. You and your friends are not magically exempt. No one knows ahead of time how hung up on it he

94

may become.

Second, a sizeable proportion of our auto accidents (and other accidents) each year are caused by drinkers. Many of these involve fatalities. These are probably otherwise nice folks, not really drunk (though some *are*), who drink enough to boost their nerve and slow their reaction time.

Third, whether or not you yourself become alcoholic or are ever involved in an accident, if you spend money for beverage alcohol, you are contributing to the availability for someone who *will* have problems.

Fourth, even the cheaper brands cost money you could be spending on something more lasting and less fattening.

Fifth, other people won't understand your drinking. You will likely have a constant battle of hide-and-seek with your parents and church friends. Many of them will be disillusioned if they discover you drink. Others may be encouraged by your example and begin something they later find they can't handle. If you remember Paul's discussion of meat offered to idols, you remember how important he felt it was to protect weaker Christians. Look up this discussion in Romans 14 and/or 1 Corinthians 8. See what principles are applicable to your drinking decision.

Our society is a fast-moving society. (It's hard to wreck a camel!) You have multiple relationships. You must make quick and accurate decisions. You will handle sophisticated and dangerous machinery. If dangerous in ancient Palestine, think what a threat it is in the United States today!

Here is a chance for you to apply authentic morality. In the spirit of chapter 14½, a legalistic answer won't solve your problem. You have a given situation which I may or may not have described accurately. What does loving God with all your heart, soul, and mind, and your neighbor as yourself say to you about drinking intoxicants?

It's the attitude of the times for college students to drink wine and smoke pot. But I hope you don't feel you have to conform.

You don't need to be coerced. You are free in Christ to live as he leads. Make your decision in love . . . for you and your friends.

16 How Should a Christian View Dating?

Steve

Isn't love wonderful? (You may well ask . . .)

"Zatchu, Doris?" says the tinny voice over the dorm telephone. "How's about popping over to the Pipsqueak Pantry wimme for a Wienie Waffle?"

"Oh, my," you think. (You, lucky thing, are Doris.) "Oh, arg, ech, blech," you think. "Oh, Arnold." Then the heavy thought comes in through the window at you. Heavy, heavy, heavy weighs the still small voice. *Why am I here?* But your computer-like mind can handle it. Click, click, comes the printout:

(1) To have fun.

(2) To get married.

(3) To learn.

Your mind returns to Arnold. "Shore, kiddo," you answer. "Come git me."

"Oh, my," Arnold whispers. "Isn't love wonderful?"

You hang up. And maybe by the time you put on your Shiny Whiny lipstick it occurs to you to wonder what love has to do with waffles, anyway.

(I am forever waiting for a rebirth of wonder about that.)

You burst into song:

Love and waffle, love and waffle;
Why the devil isn't love unlawful?
Anytime you date me
I'd prefer that you just hate me.

And I, Don Juan that I am not, hesitate to *ask* you anything, but ask I must. "Uh, what does love have to do with dating anyway?" (You don't have to be Doris anymore. Answer for yourself.)

Let me work myself toward an answer. First, let me make it clear that contrary to popular opinion, I am not the World's Greatest Lover. So I am not here to teach you techniques for getting yourself some good lovin', so to speak. I *am* here, again contrary to popular opinion, as a Christian; and it seems to me that a Christian ought to see dating differently from a secularized society. (Are you serious? you may ask. "Yes," I answer seriously, looking you straight in those fine, sensitive eyes. "Finally, yes.")

An unbeliever's basic motivation in dating is pleasure. There are finer emotions involved in the process, but even the literature of romance itself teaches us that romantic "love" is ultimately selfish and pleasure-oriented. Growing up in a hedonistic society, we tend to accept its dating patterns without questioning.

But a Christian's motivation in dating ought to be love—I don't mean romantic or erotic "love," but Christian love, *agape* (1 Corinthians 13) love which is an expression and manifestation of the love of Christ. We ought to date in order to develop relationships in which something of God exists in the space between us and our dates. I think it's bogus to say that we ought to practice a separate species of love in dating. The Bible does not teach us to practice *eros* per se, and it is a cop-out to say that biblical norms for love do not apply to our relationships with dates.

Now, I'm afraid that this view of Christian dating is not too widely held. It's simply because Doris is not interested in loving Arnold in any way, form, or fashion. She just wants the waffles. And the main reason she's in college is to have fun, not to serve God.

When you get two Christians together trying to have fun, you can get some pretty strange variations. I remember in my recently way-

97

ward youth, when I came up for air from a five-minute (honest) kiss, and that Christian girl looked at me with those big wet eyes and whispered, "Thank you, Jesus." No kidding. And I don't think that sort of thing is as uncommon as you'd expect. A friend of mine once called up the prettiest Christian girl on campus and said, "Margie, I've been praying about it; and the Lord told me he wants you to go out with me." "I'm sorry," she answered. "But he didn't tell *me* anything." Click. Some of the most excessively "spiritual" guys I know will turn their heads 360° and generally go berserk when a pretty girl walks by. It's as though their girl-watching/dating/loving-making faculties are completely cut off from their little spiritual selves. I'm sure it has something to do with the general spirit-flesh dichotomy they set up in thinking about their Christian lives. You think about that.

While I uphold the traditional Christian position on premarital sex (I'm a longtime advocate of "virginmanship"), I think that such a position should be based on a foundation of Christian love for the other member of a couple. Furthermore, in college, every date can be looked upon as a potential mate. In high school, a lot of dating is for the purpose of social learning and adjusting to patterns of male-female relationships. But for most people in college, the learning phase is over; and we need to seek God's will in developing relationships with the opposite sex.

Of course, there is plenty of room for having a good time. It would be a real drag if we could never go out with anyone but fiancé. But even the most casual dates should be thought of in a context of Christian love. We should always ask ourselves how we can deepen our relationships with our dates, how we can help them, and how we can both draw closer to God.

Bill

The Greeks had three words for it—"love," that is: *agape, eros,* and *philia.* (You've probably heard someone's interpretation of these before, but please stay; I won't be long.) *Agape* means, essentially, desiring the greatest good or placing the highest value on the object of your love. *Eros* represents affection, emotional love, sensuality, desire. *Philia* usually means friendship, comaraderie, or kinship.

Apage is mental; *eros* is emotional; *philia* is brotherly.

Agape is usually other-directed; *eros* is usually self-directed; *philia* is a mutual exchange.

Agape carries with it a deep commitment to its object. The other two are more superficial relationships.

Agape and *philia* are both biblical terms; *eros* never appears as a word in the Bible.

I say "as a word" because the idea of *eros* does appear, but that's the first thing I want to say about female-male relationships for a Christian, especially dating. When a relationship progresses to a significant level of interaction, all three types of love are normally present . . . and probably should be.

Agape should underlie all of our relationships with others. As we've said earlier, Christian morality is based on "love" for persons—placing supreme value on them (God is a person, also). A date (or any person of the opposite sex) is no exception. When Paul said, "There is neither Jew nor Greek, there is neither slave nor free, there is neither male nor female; for you are all one in Christ Jesus" (Gal. 3:28, RSV), I know he meant all were equal in the *agape* of God and should be in one another's *agape*—there should be no discrimination on the basis of sex.

I know he didn't mean there was no difference between a man and a woman; even in a robe-and-sandals culture, he knew better than that. I don't think he meant that there was no room for *eros*, for *eros* is no respecter of clothing or culture. It is so human that to deny it is to deny part of your humanity.

This doesn't mean *eros* should control your life; it should not. *Agape* should. It does mean that a part of a normal female-male relationship is *eros* love. It has to do with the genes . . . and what they produce. As some Frenchman (you'd know it!) has said, "Men and women are different, *vive le difference*!"

Eros is all through the Bible because it is a part of the persons God created. When God created Eve, Adam (Hebrew: "man") knew immediately that God had given him more than just another farmer. God had given him someone to call forth his total personality—someone to value and help (*agape*), to cherish and excite (*eros*), to share and work with (*philia*).

But let's not leave out *philia*. One of the aspects of dating that bothers me the most is the idea that every significant boy-girl relationship must be romantic, must be leading toward living together. There is a place for deep companionship between a woman and man which can be extremely supportive and enriching to both—like having a brother or sister with whom you really "synch." This kind of nonromantic relationship, by the way, is not a bad way to find out from a real one how people of the opposite sex see you . . . as a person and as a dating possibility.

And perhaps *philia* (I hope I'm not overdoing this) is that ingredient of commonality, comradeship, value-agreement that helps dates and marriages be interesting, growth-producing, and, in case of marriages, enduring.

Real love is not simple; it involves the whole person. It is *agape, eros,* and *philia*, all three, all *three*; but the greatest of these is *agape* (but you need them all). Grady Nutt coined a word for marriage love which I like: "agaperos."

More about *eros* in chapter 18. Right now, let's get back to Arnold (who seemed too full of it) and Doris (who didn't seem to have much toward Arnold).

Let's assume Doris was trying to act on Christian principles. If all she wanted from the date was waffles, should she let Arnold spend his money and time? Perhaps *not*, if she is going to be bored and act it. She will kill her evening and perhaps his ego. Perhaps *so*, if she is willing to help him also have a good time and feel better about himself. I'm sure the Christian perspective has something to say about dating the unlovely. I can't say exactly what. I know a "yukky" relationship can be deteriorating to you. It can become an awful alliance. But give the matter some thought. Along the way a lot of Christian lovers (*agape*) have helped some "frogs" to fly.

I have a problem with what may be game-playing on Doris' part.

Some girls play dating games. Doris may think that if she gets to Pipsqueak with Arnold, she will be able to see (and be seen by) George. Depending on how she stands with George, she hopes that this may make him either (1) jealous or (2) remember she exists. Arnold and George are good friends, so she may even begin dating Arnold regularly. Then she can get to know (and be known by) George. Arnold is being used. He becomes a "thing."

Boys have a few games, too. Perhaps the most destructive is making-out-with-her-as-quickly-as-possible. This game is motivated by a desire for sexual gratification, the need to dominate, a bet with a roommate, or some other depersonalizing influence. The girl becomes an "it," a thing to be used. Even some of the words boys use of girls—"chick," "broad," "bod," "date," "old lady"—are depersonalizing.

That really is what is wrong with a lot of 360° looks (see above). They are interested in only certain parts of the girl—not the whole person. Nothing wrong about admiring beauty, even if it's the female gender. The problem comes when you begin to see her as a potential gratifier of you or when you downgrade her in your mind as being essentially "body."

You have needs. Other students have needs. Some of these are pretty basic to your existence as a person: attention, security, acceptance, success, pleasure. The needs may be legitimate. But it is not difficult for a man or woman in a dating relationship to use the other to meet his own needs. The Christian emphasis on love, however, calls for relationships to be constructive, to build self-esteem and partner-esteem, to call out and encourage development of the other's total personality. If *agape* and *philia* don't develop along with *eros* in the relationship, chances are you're going to end up with a sex-centered relationship. Your being where you are in the development process, approaching the height of your sexual drives, and having a normal interest in such things, *eros* can quickly take over and short-circuit the development of a complete relationship.

Dating is an important extracurricular activity. Settling on a mate may well be the most important deciding you do at college.

But even if your dating doesn't lead to immediate matrimony, it's a great way to get to know yourself and others. It causes you to be resourceful in conversing and in thinking of interesting entertainment. It gives you a chance to know how someone else thinks and feels.

If you're a girl and haven't had much opportunity to date, I hope you don't get to feeling edgy. You have your own unique timetable of heterosexual relationships. It won't hurt, though, to make yourself as attractive as you can be without being fakey. I was talking with a male student sometime ago, a good guy. I was observing that it's the inner self that is the real person, not the looks. He agreed very matter-of-factly.

"That's right," he said. "I'm attracted to a girl first by her looks. But then I try to get to know what she's really like."

You don't have to feel embarrassed or sneaky about coming out with a new hairdo, contacts, braces, or a slimmer waistline. Some things you can't control; get going on those you can. This kind of care comes under loving (*agape*, putting supreme value on) yourself, as you do others.

Steve: Well, Bill, you seem to have made a pretty good case for *eros.* I just want to state right here that I am emphatically in favor of *eros.* Anyone who wants proof can write me, in care of Broadman Press, Nashville.

Bill: I had hoped we wouldn't have any commercials.

Steve: I agree with you that *agape, filia,* and *eros* should coexist in a dating relationship. I've tried to tell that to my dates for years. But frankly, I am skeptical of trichotomizing love. Layman that I am, it's my feeling that splitting love into three parts is more Greek than Christian. The Hebrews used only one basic word for love in the Old Testament, and I don't see that the new covenant requires a schizophrenia. When I love someone, I love them emotionally, brotherly, and God-ly. It seems to me that love is love, and then there's the phenomena of physical arousal which may or may not coincide with love. You might see how this relates to my statement, in chapter 14½, that God is love.

Bill: The problem with the word *love* is that used without explanation it means so many different things to people. The Greek helps me think a little more clearly about it.

A person *does* love with a combination of these ingredients. The combination varies from person to person and from time to time in the same person, and you can't analyze it on a percentage basis. I think of *agape*, though, as being an enduring bent of the mind that values persons as persons regardless of their personal affinity (*philia*) or emotional affection (*eros*) for them.

I'll bet you love a lot of people that you don't feel *eros* toward. I do. You probably love a lot of people you don't have much affinity for (*philia*), too.

Concerning your statement about God's love, is your point that God's perfect love has no physical arousal in it, so ours shouldn't either?

Steve: Oh, no! What kind of weirdo do you think I am? I'm just saying that simple physical arousal does not necessarily denote the presence of love. While physical arousal may accompany love and intensify it, the body can also get aroused without participating in real love which is a manifestation of God in the world. You suppose that I want to quash the body, but I want to integrate the spirit and the body. I believe in the unity of body and spirit, and in the essential unity of God which might imply the unity of love, if love is the substance by which we know him.

Also, I concede that I don't feel erotic toward *everybody*. But this may be because I have for too long attempted to categorize my relationships in accordance with the Greek Three. I would suggest that perfect love would be a fusion of the three loves, that *agape* should not be devoid of affinity and emotional elements. This is an idealization, but were such an ideal ingrained, it would not permit us to love dates in the lopsidedly erotic way now common.

17 What About Dating Within the Christian Fellowship?

Steve

Let us suppose that Doris and Arnold (the stars of chapter 16) are both Christians. That supposition immediately complicates things terribly.

"Roioioinguh," goes the phone. (You be Doris.) You can tell from the way it rings that it's Arnold. Pick up the receiver, anyway.

"Groovy, Doris, we had such a wowie time praying over the Wienie Waffles at the Pipsqueak Pantry the other night. I just had to tell you that somehow there hovering over thos waffles was, uh, love. Praise the Lord, huh . . . whatcha thinka that, Doris?"

Well, well, I reckon poor little you don't know *what* to think of that, do you? It could be this guy's in love with you; it could be he's just lonely; it could be he really felt a spiritual union. You've got to say something . . .

"Sure, *brother*," you say, emphasizing "brother" the way you would say, "Sure, *sucker*." You feel like spelling it out for him: b-r-o-t-h-e-r. "Sure, brother, praise God that we are one in the Spirit." *Not in the flesh*, you keep thinking, not in the flesh.

"Well, sister," Arnold says, the way you would say, "Well, dahlin'." "Well, sister, we need a lot of fellowship so we can grow.

How's about truckin' back over to the Pipsqueak Pantry wimme tonight? They've got a special on Pancho Pancako, with chili sauce. It's really hot stuff (ha, ha). How's about it, Doris? There's some stuff I wanna talk to ya about. You know, spiritual stuff."

You just can't get up for it now. "I'm sorry, Arnold," you gulp, "but I'm really busy tonight. I'm working on a bio lab on the effects of inbreeding in church mice."

"How interesting!" says Arnold. "Could I just watch? You won't hear a squeak outa me . . ."

The situation is classic, but I'm afraid it's usually not as funny as I've made it out to be. I must admit, once more, that I am hardly an expert in this field. In fact, there are several girls who would laugh themselves silly if they heard I was trying to give advice on this question, because I led them on indefinitely with ambiguities of statement and action, leading to problems which were less than hilarious. Perhaps the best I can do is to give you a warning. Try to be aware of confusion between brother-sister love and love which leads to dating and marriage.

This confusion is likely to occur in a healthy Christian community on campus. In such a community, there is frequent expression of affection among the members, although this is usually assumed to be a brotherly sort of affection. It should also be true that male-female love, "romantic" love, in such a community takes on the characteristics of Christian love. I think it is good that the expressions of love become similar.

Problems come, however, when a person's intentions are misunderstood by another. These misunderstandings lead to situations in which a person can injure another without meaning to. These misunderstandings have intensified in recent years since there has been a lot of "touchy-feely" sort of "relating" in Christian groups. The only way to avoid misunderstandings is clear communication with complete honesty. I saw a TV show recently in which an old-time country preacher asked a member of his congregation: "Miss School-teacher, may I have permission to court you?" That seemed silly at first, but it's really not such a bad idea. It wouldn't hurt for you to make your intentions equally clear.

Problems also come when Christians "break up." There really shouldn't be any violent romance-ending between Christians, and you need to remember that you are still one in Christ with your ex. The community as a whole needs to make an effort to avoid awkward statements and make the transition period as comfortable as possible.

Bill

Sometimes a close community like a church or campus religious group can unwittingly cause problems for those in the group who want to date. Beginning at junior high level, it seems, your friends jump at the chance to pair you off with someone. Sometimes this happens after only a date or two. It's some kind of a love-in-bloom complex. Or perhaps Gestalt psychology has a theory for it: We are unhappy when a person walks alone; when two singles become a couple, we find closure and can relax.

This makes it dangerous to date. You might get paired off permanently in everyone's mind and a breakup would hit them like a divorce. You know people will feel sorry for one or the other or both of you and give you those sad looks. I feel sure that a lot of people have married with serious doubts rather than fight the fellowship.

It gets hairy, also, when you've dated one person in the fellowship awhile, gotten yourselves fixed in everyone's mind, break up, and then start to date someone else in the group. Yet these sorts of trial relationships are what dating is all about.

I don't know what to suggest, really. If the group is small enough, initiate a formal discussion in church school or in the campus fellowship. Set your own ground rules. If you are part of a church which is too large to involve in the discussion, at least you can understand one another in your group.

A second way to soften the blow is to decide, in the event of a breakup, how you're going to handle it so you will cause the least pain to everyone. I know "the movies don't do it that way," but you can practice a little Christian maturity at this point.

Couples who show a lot of affection in public intensify the

106

breakup problem for everyone. They should have finished with this sort of behavior in high school.

Sometimes the fellowship has a way of postponing dating. A boss I had used to say of a single guy in our company, "Bob will never get married; he gets all the female companionship he needs from his fellow workers." I don't know if that was true. If so, I doubt if Bob's needs were very great. But it is true that the Christian fellowship which provides plenty of social contact can lessen the need for one-to-one dating. You just do everything together. As much as some of you would like it to be otherwise, you can't seem to break up the old gang. This kind of fellowship is extremely important. But so is dating. Fellows, the girls are usually more perceptive at this point. Don't wait until your last semester to start narrowing down your own personal fellowship.

The opposite of this can also be a problem. If people in the group begin to pair off and want to be alone or in dating couples, it can sometimes deplete the fellowship or leave a few singles staring at one another. If you're in a group like this, it may be time to have a discussion or to mention the problem individually to the dating couples. Alone time is important; but the larger fellowship is vital, also.

Take a look at what's happening in your group. Get other members to help you analyze the situation. If the need warrants it, why not begin a series of discussions on "Dating Patterns Within Our Group: Why There Aren't Any" or something else equally appropriate.

18 How Can I Relate to Students with Different Standards for Sexual Behavior?

Steve

Let us suppose that Doris and Arnold are finally out on a date, driving to the Pipsqueak Pantry. (You re-suppose you are Doris.)

"Shoeslap, shoeslap, shoeslap," go the windshield wipers. And it is not even raining. But it sure is dark, you think.

You are already on the main street. Click. Suddenly, on go the headlights. "Whisker-friskers, Doris," whimpers Arnold. "I *knew* something was wrong, but gee-jelly-banana, I thought it was just me."

"It *was* you, Arnold," say you.

"What was me, Doris?" he asks, breathing hard. "The man of your dreams was me? The voice you heard calling in the night was me?"

"No, Arnold," you reply. "What was wrong, bobo, that's what was you."

He is staring farther on down the road. He whispers: "Wow, that's heavy, Doris."

"Arnold," you say sharply, "are you feeling nervous about something?"

"Golly-jamocha no, Doris. What would I be nervous about?"

The car turns sharply to the right into a dark alley. "Ar-nold," you sing out, "where are we going, Arnold?" The car comes to a screeching halt.

"To a closer relationship, Doris."

"Oh, Arnold!"

"Holy union, Doris. I thought if you loved me in the Lord, we ought to express that love and get to know each other better."

"Oh, arg, ech, blech," you are thinking. "Oh, Arnold . . ."

This is another classic situation in which the guy has more liberal ideas about sexual morality than the girl. I suppose most girls have found some way to handle or not handle this situation by the time they get to college. But questions of technique aside, we need to remember that Christian love ought to be the basis of all behavior in dating. It is wrong for you (Doris) to get furious at Arnold when he's probably too dumb to be aware of your moral code. You ought to try to talk to Arnold about what your standards are and how you believe Christian love should be expressed. Since Arnold is a Christian, you can appeal to the Scriptures. If Arnold were not a Christian, this would be an opportunity for witness. However, while you should maintain your moral standards, I think it would be wrong for you to give Arnold this big Christian rap when the real reason you don't want a physical relationship is because Arnold is unattractive, when you know very well you would go along with someone else.

Let's forget Doris and Arnold. I don't want to leave the impression that men are always the aggressors, always the ones with more liberal standards concerning erotic conduct. In our society, females are increasingly taking the lead, acting the role of aggressor. This can leave young men in rather peculiar situations. There was this amazing incident in my recent youth in which a younger girl asked me for a ride home from high school after a late meeting. When we got into her general neighborhood, she refused to tell me where her house was. She said that she wouldn't tell me or get out of the car until I went parking with her. I was really mad. I couldn't push her out. Finally, she directed me to an uninhabited country road. I will spare you the details, but needless to say, she finally told me where her house was.

I guess that's an extreme example, but even in such a case I should have acted in Christian love. For a good while, I had a difficult time feeling Christian love toward that girl. At least, the incident made me aware of what girls feel when guys require that they go parking. But it is really somewhat more difficult for a male in our society to uphold high moral standards in such a situation. In fact, it's downright embarrassing. You still have to try to talk it out, because it's one of those situations in which you are clearly called upon to take a stand. You should remember that the other person probably has important needs, and he/she may be interpreting a need for relationship as a need for sex.

Of course, the situation can be reversed if you're dating someone with even more conservative standards of sexual behavior than your own. Charity requires that you respect those standards and be patient. Your overaggressiveness can hurt both your relationship and your witness.

Other problems arise when friends of your own sex have sexual morals different from your own. They may frequently tell stories you find offensive, bragging about exploits. I don't think the Christian is called upon to scold his friends about such things. Let them know where you stand and don't get too excited about their stories, but be patient. If you go stomping out of the room, you're acting like a clod, not a Christian. Look for opportunities to ask questions which might point out to your friends the extent to which they treat others as sex objects, and look for opportunities to show them real love.

Bill

Back to Doris and Arnold again, eh? And Arnold *thinks* the relationship is progressing. This time he's the one who's playing games. This piece of fiction may be pretty close to life. When a relationship is allowed to continue on a superficial, impersonal basis, it may be difficult to change the tenor of it. If Doris has been stringing Arnold along to get to see George, she probably has contributed to Arnold's erroneous evaluation of their relationship.

Better to be real from the start. Pretty hard to get seduced or even seriously embarrassed by someone if she or he feels you really

110

care about him as a person. (My friend Steve, above, is an obvious exception.) The relationship has a good chance of making an upward climb if your date comes to know that life matters to you—that you're not out just for pleasure or just to trap a man (or woman) by any method available or just to be a part of the "action."

This is where *philia* (see chapter 16) can help. Find and develop some common areas of interest with your dates. The question asked of dating experts used to be: "What can a Christian do on a date? There's nothing to do but go to a movie, dance, or sit and neck." The answer was usually something like, "Keep moving."

Well, conditions have changed; but the advice is not bad, if interpreted. Don't follow the path of least resistance. Plan things of interest to do. Don't let the relationship become *eros*-centered.

A good friend of mine who was a counselor and psychology teacher at a church-sponsored college noticed a certain pattern in boy-girl relationships on his campus. The boys, he said, tended to start off a relationship on the basis of *eros*—they were interested in having sex. But as the relationship deepened toward matrimony, the boy generally became less desirous of having sexual contact with his girl friend.

The opposite was true of the girls. As the relationship developed and the girl began to love and trust the boy more, she became more willing than initially to engage in heavy lovemaking. My friend attributed this difference to the girls' greater maturity. Using our categories, the girls' love was more *agape* controlled—they tended to see the boys as persons and not things to be used.

His theory was that there were no unmarried men on campus who had matured in their concept of love. Courtship became a matter of the girl holding the boy off from sexual intimacy until he came to love her for herself. If she played his way too soon, she ran the risk that she would become merely another notch on his steering wheel. On the other hand, she ran the risk of losing by refusing; he might later be salvageable.

I don't know whether this analysis holds everywhere or not. It is something to think about. Are men the aggressors? Do they act like little boys, expecting the girls—motherlike—to set the limits and de-

111

fine the relationships? Perhaps less so than a few years ago. I hope so.

This whole discussion—my friend's example, and so forth—emphasizes the danger of game-playing and the wisdom of trying to be and communicate who you really are from the beginning. If you are already pretty deep into a relationship, begin now to talk about how you feel and how you see things. No sudden lectures or explosions if you can help it, but thoughtfully work toward getting on an honest basis.

This honest sharing is even more important if you are really getting serious about someone. If you think you have some real differences in your views about sex, read through a good book together on dating and sex. Select one that leaves room for discussion, allows you to work out your own philosophy. As you discuss, be honest about how you feel. Don't be pressured or shamed into being untrue to your feelings.

Now, back to Doris for a moment. She is looking pretty pure in today's episode (above). But how would she behave in the dark alley with George instead of Arnold? She probably doesn't really know. She may *think* she does. She's had some church training, so she probably assumes she will be able to withstand the most intimate advances and defer heavy lovemaking until marriage. But suddenly faced with the possibility of getting intimate with *George*, she may find she has no real beliefs or convictions.

Better as a Christian to update your beliefs as your experience and self-understanding change. Parked in a car on a romantic night with someone who brings your *eros* level up is not the best time to think through to convictions. Again, talk to some Christian friends. Read a good book or two. Don't fall for all the old dormitory tales about sexual intercourse being a natural function (like brushing your teeth), a necessary experimental ground for marriage fitness, a guarantee of genuine relationship, or a light, after-game recreational activity.

Don't let your *eros* get ahead of your *agape*.

19 What Should Be My Attitude Toward Homosexuals?

Steve

With the increasing visibility of homosexuals in today's society, even in the Christian community, there is a question which each of us is forced to answer. Unfortunately, our answers tend toward one extreme or another: total rejection of homosexuals as persons on the one hand, and gay libertarian permissiveness on the other. I suggest that we need to find a middle way, one which both upholds Christian standards of morality and calls us to show genuine love toward homosexual persons.

Don't get me wrong—I'm not soft on perversion. Homosexual behavior is wrong. The Bible is quite explicit about that. I've seen too much heartbreak, disgust, paranoia, and loneliness to believe any differently, anyway. But what I *am* saying, dear brothers and sisters, is that we ought to treat homosexuals as human beings, just as we treat alcoholics or drug addicts, as real people with real problems.

Of course, some homosexuals do not admit that it is a problem at all. But then, neither do the socially acceptable alcoholics or the addicts who have just started. We have a duty to help them understand their behavior *is* a problem, that it is immoral. At the same time we need to recognize that the almost unbearable arrogance with which some homosexuals defend themselves may be a result of our own lack of charity in the past. Since we have not allowed them to relate to our fellowship, they have formed their own. Like ostracized children, they have formed their own club with their own rules. The only way to demonstrate the illegitimacy of their new rules is to demonstrate the love that shows our rules to be legitimate, and to welcome them into our fellowship as persons in need.

Homosexuality sometimes becomes a problem for Christians. I am frequently surprised at which people tell me they've had problems in this area. Some of the strongest Christians I know have had to overcome feelings of homosexuality.

There are at least three factors that have contributed to an increase in self-questioning (I can only talk about males): First, the frequency of broken homes has caused confusion about sex roles. Second, many young men have rejected both strict male (John Wayne) stereotypes and the demands of liberated females for "performance" as sex objects. Third, gay liberation and increased attention on homosexuality causes young men to consider it as an alternative, especially when Christian training has taught them to avoid contact with girls and has never mentioned homosexuality. The hush-hush attitude among Christians precludes the possibility of reassurance from the community of believers. People worry about it a lot, a whole lot more than Christians are willing to recognize.

Often the best way to help a Christian who is having doubts about his sexuality is simply to reassure him that he is normal. If he doesn't have serious problems in sexual behavior, don't let him think of himself as a pervert. It is apparent that a tendency toward homosexuality can be determined by one's family background and early experiences. Such a tendency is not in and of itself a sin. One should pray that God will remove this tendency. Willed homosexual *behavior,* however, is clearly a sin; the sinner needs to ask forgiveness and to pray for psychological healing.

While accepting homosexual Christians as persons, you need to take care not to encourage any sexual advances or fantasies. What may seem mildly affectionate behavior to you might seem wildly suggestive to him. Probably one of the least helpful things you can do is to try to prove by physical contact that you are not afraid of him. You probably don't need to worry about being attacked or anything, but you may inadvertently encourage his fantasies. Still, it is crucial that you demonstrate Christian love rather than revulsion.

Bill

Some of the extreme negative feelings in our society toward homosexuality may have come out of the Judeo-Christian tradition. Homosexuality is not mentioned often in the Bible, but the few instances seem particularly strong in their condemnation.

In probably the best-known Old Testament passage (Gen. 19) we have the ultimate destruction of Sodom and Gomorrah, with the result that one type of unnatural sex act is now called *sodomy*. A similar incident is reported in Judges 19. But both of these happenings describe situations so bizarre that we can hardly develop a theology from them. Even the "good guys" seem to offer weird solutions according to our modern standards.

Perhaps the most overt reference to homosexuality in the New Testament is found in the first chapter of Romans. In describing some perversions of religion, Paul says that some worshipers of idols, animals, and images also participated in "unnatural" (Rom. 1:26) sex acts—women with women and men with men. The description seems to indicate these were deliberate homosexual acts related to the participants' worship practices. Paul says they received the logical end of their perverted worship behavior, almost complete corruption of personality. But here also the Bible is reporting a particularized condition which is not our primary concern today when we think about homosexuality.

Though not mentioned explicitly, homosexuality is probably included in the writer's mind when he lists "fornication," "uncleanness," "lasciviousness," and "inordinate affection" as works of the flesh (Rom. 6:19; Gal. 5:19; Eph. 5:3; Col. 3:6), which he says should not be found among Christians.

Again, the perfect compatibility of male and female given in the

115

Genesis creation account also emphasizes the abnormality of homosexual relationships.

So, what are we to conclude from the biblical evidence? It seems clear that homosexuality is not the God-intended relationship to fulfill and complete either the man or woman. Physically, emotionally, even spiritually, men and women seem indeed created to complement each other. The homosexual, because of his confused identity, cannot seem to attain the deep level of intimacy God intended.

A second, and related, teaching seems evident: Christians are to avoid homosexual activities. These are forbidden along with fornication, adultery, anger, jealousy, selfishness, and several others.

But it is difficult to see from this evidence that God's wrath will be visited on homosexuals in a unique judgment. A biblical case can perhaps be made between his attitude toward a deliberately cultivated homosexuality and one that is a personality characteristic. There is a predatory kind of homosexual who is deliberately out to use or pervert others, to take advantage of their age or weakness. Paul's severe denouncement seems appropriate to this person. But the same case could be made in comparing any premeditated and unpremeditated wrongs. Even here the distinction is difficult for human observers. Who can know what inner turmoil molds another's actions?

"It is hard to imagine," says pastoral counselor Andrew Lester, "the God of love rejecting human beings because of the psychological condition of homosexuality anymore than he would reject an individual suffering from emotional illness or retardation. Just because homosexual people fall short of their human potential does not mean they are outside of God's mercy and acceptance." (*Sex Is More Than a Word*, Nashville: Broadman Press, 1973, p. 84.)

This is no defense of homosexuality. It recognizes that it falls short of God's will for persons. But it raises a question about the way our society often treats homosexual persons. Homosexuals are ridiculed, stigmatized, blackmailed, physically beaten, threatened, and sometimes deprived of their civil rights. This kind of treatment fails to recognize the cause of the problem. It also makes it extremely difficult for a person who suspects he has homosexual tendencies to get help. Too much is at stake if even a suspicion is aroused.

Experts do not agree on the causes of homosexuality. Some research seems to support the theory that heredity may be a factor—particularly the functioning of glands and the balance of hormones. Other authorities believe homosexuality develops in childhood when a child overidentifies with the parent of the opposite sex.

Whatever the earlier reasons, it seems clear that homosexual tendencies grow during adolescence when a young person fails to develop adequate heterosexual relationships. There can be several reasons for this failure. An adolescent may feel physically unattractive. He may have experienced embarrassment or awkwardness in his attempts at boy-girl relating. He may think of himself as unlikeable or uninteresting. Or he or she may have strong emotional revulsion to members of the opposite sex—fear, uneasiness, hostility. Any of these experiences can lead a person to turn for affection to a less threatening person of his or her own sex.

As Andrew Lester points out, it is important to distinguish between *having a homosexual experience* and *being a homosexual.* Some people worry about some adolescent homosexual feeling or experience marking them as being homosexual. Others are concerned that their physical characteristics—masculinity in women, effeminacy in men—mean that they are homosexual. But these experiences or traits in themselves are not signs of homosexuality. Many female homosexuals, for instance, are very feminine; many male homosexuals are muscular and athletic.

Lester says that "you should be concerned about your sexual identity if you (1) center your strongest affection on friends of the same sex and never feel any affection toward members of the opposite sex, (2) if you frequently desire to view the nude bodies of members of your own sex, (3) if you fantasize or daydream continously about homosexual relationships, or (4) if you desire frequent physical contact and anticipate playing with the genitals of members of the same sex." (*Sex Is More Than a Word*, pp. 88 f.)

Contrary to some popular opinion, homosexual feelings can be helped toward heterosexuality. Psychiatrists, clinical psychologists, doctors, and counselors who can help best are nearly always available in a college community. If you, or anyone you know, find yourselves leaning toward homosexuality, or even if you are concerned about your sexuality, you may want to talk with one of these professionals. But perhaps you merely need to relate more to persons of the opposite sex.

20 What About Marriage?

Steve

Arnold once asked me this question, and I just laughed. I'm afraid some of my friends would laugh to hear me ask this question, too. More than one has said to me, "If you *ever* decide to get married, let me know. I'm dying to meet the girl who can catch little Stevie." Well, so am I. But needless to say, in my condition of inexperience and naivete, I am hardly an expert on marriage. I'll just raise a few questions and let the old man handle them.

First of all, you have to ask yourself if you should get married at all. In our society, it's almost accepted to remain single. There are, at any rate, increasing numbers of single young adults who form a large circle of acceptance. You shouldn't just assume that you'll get married; you should pray about it and consider your alternatives.

There are a lot of legitimate questions to ask yourself here: Can I serve God more efficiently if I am single? Do I want to bring children into this world? Can I cope with my sexuality if I remain single? What are my motivations for wanting to be married? Is there anyone around I can really picture myself married to in twenty years?

I've noticed that nowadays Christian student couples tend to get married quicker than unbelievers. This is a bit strange. I suppose the reason is that non-Christian couples don't see any need to get married since they often live together without legal ties. And so, cynic that I am, it seems to me that the reason Christian couples get married earlier is because they feel a need to legitimatize sex. I really question whether that is a good enough reason to get married while in school. I think we've got to come to a more mature understanding of what a marriage is for, of the responsibilities that we must accept, of the strain that this can be on our studies, and of what God wants for us.

"Old Man"

It was a bit of a shock to me at first. But the idea has grown on me—the idea that you don't have to get married at twenty-two. If this change of style is to avoid responsibility, I don't care for it. If it makes sex too casual and pleasure-focused, that's unfortunate. I can think of some bad aspects to this trend.

But I like the fact that the present young adult culture is making room for singles, that getting married is not something you must do before you graduate, that the drive to matrimony is perhaps not carrying everything before it as it once did. This new atmosphere does give you room to decide whether or not marriage is for you. Hopefully it will help you to choose your mate more carefully. Incidentally, it may aid the overpopulation situation.

If it delays your marriage, it may help you. Several people I know who are getting divorces apparently didn't know themselves or each other well enough when they married. Perhaps a later marriage would have given some of them more opportunity for knowing.

Still, people change. No matter when you marry, you can be a different person a year later. This generation of youth and young adults are in some ways the most mature the world has known. Why wouldn't early marriage work?

The truth is that many (most) college marriages *do* work. Grades, health, attitudes, and maturity all improve for most students when they get married—provided they can handle their finances without overwork and don't have children too soon.

In many ways, college is a beautiful time to get married. You are physiologically old enough. You are flexible. You can acquire mutual friends—maybe the most lasting you'll ever have. You can have an early start toward developing similar tastes, values, and interests. You have opportunity to grow up together.

But there's another truth. Statistics show that the older persons are when they marry, the more lasting their marriage. As someone has said, marriage is for the mature. Problems are going to come up—with finances, in-laws, sex, goals, life-styles—and the more experienced, understanding persons can usually handle them more easily. A challenging job, a bank account, established community relationships—the steadying conditions usually accompanying later marriage—have their values.

I suppose the ideal time for marriage is when you are old enough to know who you are and what your goals are and young enough to bend a little, so the *two* can become *one*.

Given these conditions, probably the greatest asset a marriage can have is commitment. I had a teacher in theological seminary who said (unbelievably to me, a one-year groom at the time) that if he and his wife hadn't pledged themselves to stay married, they would have divorced on several occations. I'm sure he meant it. From what I have heard, read, and experienced, almost all couples have at times differences and/or difficulties so severe that they can easily justify divorce. Only the commitment to each other, to God, and to some idea of marriage has kept them together.

This is not to say that "all marriages are made in heaven," whatever that means. In spite of everything, some of the most unlikely (and unlike) couples make it. With God's help, yes; but mostly through *working at it*: listening and hearing, being thoughtful, helping each other, talking things out, showing affection, being interesting, staying alive—changing. This is what *agape* means in a marriage. This is the kind of love that endures.

To have a chance, of course, a couple needs to have a certain amount of common ground, though it's hard to say that any one thing is absolutely essential . . . unless it's a willingness to communicate. Many other things are important: educational level, religious faith, family background, personality characteristics, attitude toward money, attitude toward sex, concepts of male-female roles, and so forth.

Because Steve and I don't spend much space on these doesn't mean they're not important. A wide discrepancy at any of these points can cause serious difficulties. I am always fearful of the future of a marriage, for instance, where a high-school-graduate wife works her husband through college and maybe grad school, without furthering her own education; the couple is building up a critical educational-interest gap.

In our day of rising recognition of women's rights, a couple needs some basic agreement at the point of female-male roles. They need to be committed to helping each other achieve personal fulfillment. This must include some common understanding about what this will mean in terms of work, housekeeping, having children, bank accounts, and so forth.

Many personality quirks are livable and redeemable. But some are not easily accommodated in a marriage. Unfortunately in the rosy hue of courtship some serious personality problems are overlooked or dismissed as unimportant. A friend who was going through some marital difficulties remarked dead earnestly: "If I ever get married again, I'm going to insist we both have thorough psychological testing before we get too serious." Pretty realistic. But fairly unromantic . . . and therein lies its drawback for most American "to-be's." They don't want to risk losing the sentimental glow.

A counselor, counseling pastor, campus minister, or trained medical doctor can help you recognize your tendencies without destroying your romance. Even if you go on with the marriage, at least you will know what you will need to work on.

A question you may be asking in the light of modern changes in marriage patterns: Am I assuming monogamous, one-time-for-life marriages as the Christian ideal? Yes, I am. I may not be up-to-date, but it seems to me that only with this kind of relationship can a person have the atmosphere of commitment, trust, and freedom in which to grow. *Agape* love demands the offer of commitment, trust, and freedom in marriage. Even Christian communes tend to move in this

122

direction.

The nuclear family, however, is another matter. "Nuclear family" is used commonly to mean a family of one wife and mother, one husband and father, their children, and no more. We have been moving toward this definition of family in the West for many years. So much so that you and I may have difficulty thinking of any other kind of "family." But if you ever saw *The Waltons* on TV, you observe a slightly different family makeup—a set of grandparents were a part of "the family."

There are some obvious values to be gained from sharing insights and responsibilities in this way. More family adults with whom the children can identify are around. More stored-up wisdom is available on call. Expenses can be shared. Perhaps the family was never intended to be as isolated as it usually is in our society. Those experiments going on in our society now to denuclearize the family may contribute significantly to its ultimate health.

Note, so far I have not referred to any biblical material except the obligation to love, *agape*-style. One reason is that the same sort of cultural lag between then and now is as obvious in marriage customs as it is in drinking customs. The creation account implies one wife for one husband. But in the early Old Testament, the patriarchs had both wives and concubines. Sarah gave Abraham permission to have a child by her servant Hagar. Jacob took to wife two daughters of the same man, Laban. Solomon had many wives. Though we don't have many details, it's likely that this pattern persisted through the entire period covered by the Old Testament writings. During much of this period, women were thought of as possessions of men, perhaps more so than as companions.

The New Testament is more monogamous, but it is not as enthusiastic about marriage as you might suppose. Some places it seems to favor nonmarriage (1 Cor. 7:1-9, 26-35). The two dominant persons of the New Testament—Jesus and Paul—were both bachelors. Peter's mother-in-law is mentioned, but otherwise no reference is made to any disciple's being married. As far as we can tell Mary, Martha, and Lazarus were all single. At one point, when asked who his family was,

Jesus pointed to his fellow believers.

Jesus had some things to say about divorce—like, that men couldn't just up and put a woman away without good reason (fornication was the only one he mentioned)—but not much about marriage. In this connection he quotes Genesis 2:24 to indicate that God's original plan was to have a man and a woman leaving their parents and becoming "one flesh."

Paul, particularly in his earlier writings, seems to discourage marriage. He seems to see marriage as fragmenting a person's loyalty, which should go only to God (1 Cor. 7:26-35). Apparently Paul also expected Jesus' return to be immediate; marriage, therefore, would only get in the way.

Throughout the New Testament, however, the major writers recognize the existence and importance of families and prefer the monogamous state. Both Jesus and Paul made their abode with families. In Paul's later writings, he listed being "the husband of only one wife" as being a qualification for both deacon and pastor (1 Tim. 3:12). He compared the relationship of bride and groom to that of the church and of Christ, implying among other things that marriage should be a powerful symbol of a faithful covenant (Eph. 5:31 f.).

Paul seemed to mellow toward marriage in his later writings. In a beautiful passage in his letter to both the Ephesians (5:22 to 6:4) and the Colossians (3:18-21), he gives instructions to family members about loving and caring for one another.

In summarizing the explicit biblical references to marriage, one scholar observed that the biblical family was much more an open community than the modern white American family is today. People opened their homes to travelers and entertained strangers. Early Christian homes were the only church buildings the first-century communities had.

"The family was not simply a way for two people of different sexes to meet each other's needs and the needs of their children," says John Snow, professor at Episcopal Theological School in Massachusetts. "It was part of a community [the church] committed to meeting the deprivation of the world, spiritual and physical." (John Snow,

124

"Christian Marriage and Family Life," *Christianity and Crisis*, Vol. 33, No. 23, January 7, 1974, p. 281.) It also received the rich spiritual and emotional support of the community of which it was a part. It was not left to sink or swim on its own resources alone.

The family was a model of faithfulness to one another, but it realized even a higher loyalty—it was to serve God and its fellows. Perhaps this is what Jesus was saying when he said, "If anyone comes to me and does not hate his own father or mother and wife and children and brothers and sisters, yes, and even his own life, he cannot be my disciple" (Luke 14:26, RSV).

The family was important. He who neglected to support his family was "worse than an unbeliever" (1 Tim. 5:8, RSV). But the family was not to be worshiped; only God could have first place.

21 To What Extent Should I Get Involved in Political and Community Affairs?

Steve

I can't answer this question for you specifically, since I don't know your situation: the needs around you and your gifts to meet those needs. I do think we need to make it clear that Christian morality involves politics as well as decisions about personal matters.

As evangelical Christians we have tended recently to downplay the importance of politics and secular institutions in general. We act as if the kingdom of God we live in were completely divorced from the world, as if our citizenship in that realm precludes any responsibility in this secular one. This may be because we are afraid that we cannot compete in the "real" world, or because we see we are happier in our world than "they" are in "theirs." Or, it may be because of genuine misunderstanding of our mission in the world as disciples of Christ.

We must recognize that in a democracy the authority ordained by God is *us*. In a government of the people, we the people are the ones to whom God has given the responsibility for governing. If the government is ineffective, we cannot blame God, or the Romans as Paul could; we must blame ourselves. Post-Watergate disillusionment may lead us to a healthy skepticism of man and his institutions. I'm not saying that we should all be politicians. That depends on the gifts God has given you and the needs in your community. I *am* saying that as voters we have a duty to be informed, at least. There is no excuse for a Christian student who doesn't even know where the latest war is going on. How can we turn our country toward a Christian morality, how can we even pray intelligently, if we are not informed?

Some of us say that we don't have time to get involved in politics. This may be true. However, we need to see such an involvement as a ministry, just as valid as any other ministry. We may be able to save a lot of lives and feed a lot of people by political ministry. We should not try to weigh our secular responsibilities against our religious ones. We should weigh all our opportunities for ministry, including political involvement, against one another. Then we need to consider our gifts and pray to know God's will.

Bill

One of the reasons I think students should be involved in church and a campus religious organization is because most of them offer—in the form of social action or missions projects—opportunities to help people in obvious need. After struggling to make sense of your academic work and trying to witness to a disinterested roommate and dealing with the problems of affluence on and off campus, you can be personally refreshed and uplifted by helping someone who knows he needs help.

Campus life tends to be circular—it revolves around itself. Both professors and students are notorious for getting lost in their own provincial world. The big football game is more important than war in the Middle East. The cafeteria food is more disturbing than the curtailment of the public school free lunch program. "Bangladesh" sounds like a new shish kabob place across campus. Kissinger is a communicative disease being treated in the health center.

It sometimes takes effort to remind yourself that there is a real world out there where the people have needs much different from yours . . . and perhaps much more severe. But Christian morality involves much more than what you do on a date or how you write a term paper. It includes your concern about how people are affected by their environment—their schools, their employment, their government. Authentic morality is concerned about how persons are doing.

Jesus was amazing in being able to relate to all sorts of people—the rich young ruler, Nicodemus, the woman at the well, the woman taken in adultery, Mary, Martha, Lazarus, Matthew the tax collector, blind Bartimaeus, the man who called himself Legion, several fishermen, a wild-eyed revolutionary. He loved them all. But the ones to whom his heart and life really extended were those who could not help themselves: the children, the women, the lepers, the lame, the possessed—the humble of the earth, the common folk.

Jesus seemed to give his time—all day, every day—helping these persons: healing, encouraging, listening, forgiving, inspiring, befriending, teaching, preaching. You can tell where his concern was, by those he ached for:

> Blessed are the poor in spirit, for theirs is the kingdom of heaven.
> Blessed are those who mourn, for they shall be comforted.
> Blessed are the meek, for they shall inherit the earth.
>
> . . . .
> Blessed are the pure in heart, for they shall see God.

(Matt. 5:3-8, RSV)

This concern of *his* puts the pressure on *you* . . . to remember and to help the deprived of our world anyway you can . . . to make the most of your opportunity to study and learn . . . to dedicate this training to the present and the ultimate betterment of as many persons as possible.